THE NEW LIFE

Talks with Christians on Practical Victory

By
Captain Reginald Wallis

Foreword by: Dr. Charles G. Trumbull
Introduction by: Dr. Charles R. Solomon
Edited by: Dr. John B. Woodward

THE NEW LIFE
Original Edition: 1932
GFI Edition, 2002

Published by
Grace Fellowship International
P. O. Box 368
Pigeon Forge, TN 37868   USA

www.GraceFellowshipIntl.com
Phone: (865) 429-0450

ISBN 978-0-9668312-4-5

Printed by
Lightning Source Inc.
1246 Heil Quaker Blvd.
La Vergne, TN 37086 USA
www.lightningsource.com

Scripture quotations (unless indicated otherwise) are from
The Holy Bible, King James Version

Table of Contents

APPENDICES

The New Life

Foreword

There are three tenses in the Gospel: past, present, and future; and the present tense is the part of the Gospel with which Christian people, in general, seem to be least familiar. We all know that when we receive Christ as Savior, our past sins are dealt with and blotted out, and that when we die, or when the Lord comes again, we shall be forever with Him. Past and future, therefore, are blessedly provided for in the Gospel. But what about the present?

Comparatively few Christians have dared to believe that they have a Savior who is just as able and just as faithful in providing a miraculous experience of salvation in the *present tense*, now and here while we are on earth, as He has done for our past and will do for our future. But this present tense of the Gospel is a vital part of the Good News, and it is what many children of God are now thanking Him for because they were led to see it at a Victorious Life Conference. The Victorious Life is the Gospel in the present tense.

It is made luminously clear and powerfully convincing in this greatly needed book by Captain Wallis. His ministry at America's Keswick (Keswick Grove, New Jersey) has been greatly blessed to many as it has in his own city, Dublin, and elsewhere in Great Britain. There is nothing new in the wonderful truths given here; the British Keswick has held them forth for more than half a century past, and they have been known, believed, accepted, and rejoiced in ever since the Holy Spirit first gave them to the apostle Paul and other writers of the inspired Scriptures, both New Testament and Old. But the truth of victory in this present life is utterly new to every one who sees and enters into it for the first time; then, indeed, realizing that he is *a new creation: Old things are passed away; behold, all things are beome new* (2 Corinthians 5:17).

The testimony and teaching of Captain Wallis are to be welcomed indeed, and are sure to be a channel of blessing to many who read it, for they are based on the inviolable Word of

God, of which its Author says: *It shall not return unto Me void, but it shall accomplish that which I please, and it shall prosper in the thing whereto I sent it* (Isaiah 55:11). And God Himself describes what it is He pledges Himself to accomplish: *For ye shall go out with joy, and be led forth with peace: the mountains and the hills shall break forth before you into singing, and all the trees of the field shall clap their hands. Instead of the thorn shall come up the fir tree, and instead of the briar shall come up the myrtle tree* (Isaiah 55:12,13a).

That is the Victorious Life.

Charles G. Trumbull
Author of *Victory in Christ*

Introduction

We have used this anointed book by Captain Wallis almost since the inception of Grace Fellowship International more than forty years ago. It was a personal blessing to me as it has been to many others.

I believe it is just as timely today as it was when it was first published seventy years ago by Loizeaux Bros.; it is our conviction that it should be made available to the present generation. Dr. John Woodward, our Director, has made a valuable contribution by making the terminology more consistent (see Appendix B). He has prepared a study guide to assist the reader in exploring the book personally, in small groups, or Sunday School classes (see Appendix A).

I commend this book to you as a volume that is profoundly simple and simply profound! Captain Wallis, being dead, yet speaketh. I pray that the Holy Spirit will use these words from the past to transform your present and give you a glorious future.

Please pray that God will use this book to spark revival in our time and to bring glory to our Lord Jesus Christ.

Charles R. Solomon
President and Founder, Grace Fellowship International
Author of *Handbook to Happiness*

The New Life

Preface

Thanks be unto God, who leads me on from place to place, IN THE TRAIN OF HIS TRIUMPH, to celebrate HIS victory over the enemies of Christ (2 Corinthians 2:14, Coneybeare)

The contents of this little book present the substance of a series of addresses which the Lord graciously privileged me to give at various conferences and other gatherings of His people on both sides of the Atlantic. So numerous have been the requests that these simple messages might appear in printed form, that after much delay and hesitation, I now feel constrained in the Lord to respond to this desire. Multitudes of Christian men and women today are hungering for a sane, well-balanced, Biblical message of victory over sin and self. Some are seeking for it along avenues which lead to unscriptural extremes in "holiness" teaching, resulting oftentimes in fanaticism of a distressing nature. When the Lord Jesus dealt with the sin question at Calvary, He fully met all the righteous requirements of divine justice, completely vanquished all the believer's enemies, and thereby provided for every need of saint and sinner for time and eternity:

Great Victory over sin, and death and woe,
Which needs no second fight,
and leaves no second foe.

May the dear Lord graciously vouchsafe His unction upon these written meditations in even greater measure than He has been pleased to bless the spoken word, granting the illumination of the Holy Spirit to all honest seekers after the real and only highway to joyous, overcoming, and compelling Christian testimony.

Reginald Wallis
March, 1932

The New Life

Chapter 1

Is Constant Victory Really Possible for Every Believer?

The Question Stated

This is a vitally important question for you and me, my brother or sister in Christ. Should a Christian expect and experience constant triumph, every day and all day, over [intentional] sin and self? Is the victorious life really practical, or is it just an attractive subject for conference gatherings and an interesting topic for discussion? Is it merely a pet theme for extremists and fanatics, or is there actually a sane, Biblical experience of practical triumph within the reach of every believer, irrespective of temperament, circumstances, environment, or changing times and conditions? Is it some great ideal to which we must ever seek to aspire in the vague hope that, after years of experience or service, we may perhaps approximate to such a standard? Does the Word really promise a life of true spiritual achievement, conquest, and supremacy to the simplest and weakest believer, or has God reserved such a priceless blessing as this for only a few of His favorites?

Many Christians are asking these questions today. Faced with the never-ending antagonism of a threefold enemy—the allurements of *the world*, the insidious outworkings of *the flesh*, and the subtle devices of *the devil*—all combining in a terrible assault against the testimony of real Life, the whole matter constitutes an acute problem as to Christian ethics and the real practicability of certain doctrines and theories.

What is the Victorious Life?

Now let us consider this question simply and honestly, with minds and hearts open to the revelation of the Spirit of God. Firstly, what is the victorious life? In answering this question, it will be helpful to consider what it is *not*. It is not a creed, or dogma, or dictum, or merely a particular *line of Bible teaching*, or a system of rules and regulations, or a code of ethics, or even spiritual principles. The victorious Christian life is a PERSON (John 14:6). And that Person is the Lord Jesus Christ Himself. HE is the believer's life (John 11:25). Apart from Him there is no life for you and me in the spiritual realm. Real life finds its birth in the reception of Him as Savior. Entrance into the family of God must be by the regenerating operation of the Holy Spirit (Titus 3:5). Spiritual life is not an abstract principle, or mere objective doctrine. It is *Christ*. His advent into the heart that opens to Him is the *Alpha* of a spiritual career, for *If any man have not the Spirit of Christ, he is none of His* (Rom. 8:9). Allow the Holy Spirit to write this upon your mind and spirit with an indelible pen. It is a simple fact which calls for a new emphasis today, because there are many who are *trying to live the Christian life, before they have received the Christian life to live* (Rom. 10:3). Every believer, every Christian, every Child of God, possesses Life because such a one has received Christ (Col. 2:6), and for no other reason. Separation from Him means spiritual death (Eph. 2:1). Real Life is more than joining a church, or passing through a religious ceremony. It is not imagination, or imitation, or reformation, or confirmation, or education. It is REGENERATION, the production of *a new creation* in Christ Jesus (2 Cor. 5:17). What happens, then, when one is born again (John 3:3)? Nothing short of this: Christ HIMSELF enters (Rev. 3:20) to dwell in the heart by faith through the Holy Spirit (Eph. 3:17). The human spirit is quickened [made alive] with the very life of God. This is imperative—the first great transaction between the soul and God. Nothing less than this can lift the soul into the only realm where victory becomes a possibility.

Is Christ Divided?

Now consider, therefore: *How much* of Christ did you receive at your regeneration? When He says, *I will come in*, is there any statement or inference that He will only *partially* enter? Why, of course not! Such a suggestion is illogical and foolish. *Is Christ divided* (1 Cor. 1:13)? What sort of a Savior entered your heart, then, when you turned the handle of faith and admitted Him? The Savior of the Bible, and no other. There is only one Lord Jesus Christ, and He says, *All power is given unto Me* (Matt. 28:18). Think of it. All power is vested in the Christ of God—the Christ who lives within you. *In Him dwelleth all the fullness of the Godhead bodily* (Col. 2:9). Yes, amazing as it may appear to be, this mighty, triumphant Christ, the omnipotent Son of God, actually abides in the heart of the believer by the blessed Holy Spirit. Seek to lay hold of the implications of this glorious fact. Fix your gaze upon the PERSON of Christ. The victorious Christian life, therefore, is not a great, exalted ideal to which the believer is ever struggling to aspire. Christ Himself is your life, and since His life is a victorious life, you received all the potentialities of complete victory the very moment you received Him.

An Experiential Possibility

Here, therefore, we come to our first logical conclusion. Unceasing victory *is possible for every believer*, because that blessed One who Himself is unceasingly victorious, has entered the redeemed spirit, and that to stay. For this reason, we find that the life of fullness in God is promised on the most simple conditions. There is nothing intricate or mystical about it. Our blessed Lord said: *He that believeth* (the same simple condition as for salvation), *out of his inner man shall flow rivers of living water* (John 7:38). Is that the life of victory you are seeking? That is the life promised to every believer! Repudiate any suggestion, therefore, that the victorious Christian life is an unrealistic or fanciful theory. It is an experiential possibility. Indeed, it is the birthright of the weakest or simplest believer (Rom. 10:12). This is affirmed and reaffirmed times wtihout number in many clear pronouncements of the Word of God. Allow me to quote a few of these outstanding promises:

> *Then sang Moses and the children of Israel this song unto the LORD, and spake, saying, "I will sing unto the LORD, for he hath triumphed gloriously: the horse and his rider hath he thrown into the sea"* (Ex. 15:1).

> *And the LORD shall make thee the head, and not the tail; and thou shalt be above only, and thou shalt not be beneath; if that thou hearken unto the commandments of the LORD thy God, which I command thee this day, to observe and to do them* (Deut. 28:13).

> *There shall not any man be able to stand before thee all the days of thy life: as I was with Moses, so I will be with thee: I will not fail thee, nor forsake thee* (Josh. 1:5).

> *Thine, O LORD is the greatness, and the power, and the glory, and the victory, and the majesty: for all that is in the heaven and in the earth is thine; thine is the kingdom, O LORD, and thou art exalted as head above all* (1 Chron. 29:11).

> *And she shall bring forth a son, and thou shalt call his name JESUS: for he shall save his people from their sins* (Matt. 1:21).

> *For sin shall not have dominion over you: for ye are not under the law, but under grace* (Rom. 6:14).

> *O wretched man that I am! who shall deliver me from the body of this death? I thank God through Jesus Christ our Lord. So then with the mind I myself serve the law of God; but with the flesh the law of sin* (Rom. 7:24,25).

For the law of the Spirit of life in Christ Jesus hath made me free from the law of sin and death (Rom. 8:2).

But thanks be to God, which giveth us the victory through our Lord Jesus Christ (1 Cor. 15:57).

Now thanks be unto God, which always causeth us to triumph in Christ, and maketh manifest the savour of his knowledge by us in every place (2 Cor. 2:14).

For whatsoever is born of God overcometh the world: and this is the victory that overcometh the world, even our faith (1 John 5:4).

And they overcame him by the blood of the Lamb, and by the word of their testimony; and they loved not their lives unto the death (Rev. 12:11).

These shall make war with the Lamb, and the Lamb shall overcome them: for he is Lord of lords, and King of kings: and they that are with him are called, and chosen, and faithful (Rev. 17:14).

God's Norm

Do these Scriptures suffice to establish the fact that nothing short of steady, permanent conquest in Christ is God's norm for every believer? The defeated Christian is a monstrosity from the divine viewpoint. He is abnormal. He is a paralyzed member of the Body (1 Cor. 2:14). The vanquished child of God fails to function effectively in the divine program and purpose. Backsliding and carnality are not only inexcusable, but incompatible with normal Christian experience. They produce a regime of contradiction. Since a living Christ dwells within, there is never any reason for defeat. No enemy is too powerful for the ALMIGHTY (Ps. 91:1). Every temptation may be resisted (1 Cor. 10:13). Every emergency may be triumphantly anticipated. If a believer is overcome by the enemy, the simple explanation is that the Savior has been denied His rightful position of supremacy in the heart. His dethronement must ever lead to failure in the conflict, and an arrest of spiritual life. Since practical victory can never be divorced from His indwelling presence, therefore, it follows that the life of triumph is hopeless apart from HIM (John 15:5). Again, let me repeat—*HE IS YOUR VICTORIOUS LIFE.*

The Threefold Enemy

Now let us consider these great enemies which present their triple challenge and protest to the life of victory. They are threefold: the world (1 John 2:16); the flesh (Rom. 8:3); and the devil (1 Pet. 5:8).

1. *The World.* What is *the world* in this sense? It means *this present evil world* (Gal. 1:4)—the great system of evil round about us. It is animated by the *prince of this world* (John 14:30) and characterized by a tragic decree concerning the Man of Calvary—*We will not have this Man to reign over us* (Luke 19:14). It is the world system of rebellion against God. Now, is it possible for the believer to live a truly separated Christian life in the midst of such antagonism? For example, is Christ's victory such that there is a complete loss of appetite for worldly pleasures and pursuits, with all their alluring attractions and fascinating enticements today? Is it really possible for a present-day Christian to rejoice with the apostle Paul that he has been *crucified to the world* and the world unto him, even though he dwells in the midst of it (Gal. 6:14)? Or, is it in the will of God that, having been saved from this present evil world, he should once again be captivated by its *beggarly elements* (Gal. 4:9)? The Bible answer is clear and plain. Thank God. VICTORY IS POSSIBLE, for the Lord Jesus Christ said: *I have overcome the world* (John 16:33). Because He overcame, you also may overcome, for He is yours. Mrs. Lemmel embodies the secret in her beautiful chorus:

Turn your eyes upon Jesus,
Look full in His wonderful face;
And the things of earth will grow strangely dim,
In the light of His glory and grace.

It should be remembered also that such victory is not cruel and arduous. True victory is never a hardship to be endured. It is a life to be enjoyed and radiated. The program of the world is not refused because of a sense of bondage under a torturing yoke. Never! The blessed Lord Jesus said, *My yoke is easy* (Matt. 11:30), and so it ever proves to be. On the contrary, the way of transgressors is hard (Prov. 13:15). His commandments are not grievous (1 John 5:3). They lead to a joyous, willing, grateful liberation into the blessed will of God. Here is joy unspeakable and full of glory (1 Pet. 1:8). It is the explosive power of a new affection. Such a blessedness robs the world's farewell of any pain. Yes; ask those who know. Their unanimous verdict will be that, His yoke is easy and His burden is light, and their eternal song:

Now none but Christ can satisfy,
None other name for me;
There's love, and life, and lasting joy,
Lord Jesus, found in Thee.

2. *The Flesh.* Then, secondly, there is *the flesh.* The apostle Paul says: *I know that in me (that is, in my flesh) dwelleth no good thing* (Rom. 7:18). What is *the flesh* in this sense? The next chapter will go more fully into this important question, but suffice it to say here that *the flesh* is fallen human nature (Gen. 6:3). It is the corrupt principle of sin, which *the natural man* has inherited from his fallen parents. It is [characterized by] the Adamic nature. It is the birthplace of all those ugly sins and besetments which so easily mar the Christian's joy and hinder his testimony (Gal. 5:19). Again, can it be the will of God that, having been lifted into the realm of spiritual life and justified from sin before Him forever (Rom. 5:9), the people of God should continue to be victims of such ugly traits? The works of the flesh include:

17

- *Temper*—failure to control oneself when aroused.
- *Irritability*—the tendency to manifest impatience on little provocation.
- *Moodiness*—a capricious disposition and a yielding to temperamental weaknesses.
- *Jealousy*—the spirit of fear and revenge at the prospect of being displaced by a rival.
- *Pride*—the spirit of self-exaltation and glory.
- *Selfishness*—the *ME first* spirit, and the tendency to minister to self.
- *Unforgiveness*—the refusal to forgive.
- *Anxiety and fret*—the tendency to worry when difficulties and dangers threaten.
- *Complaining*—a grumbling, dissatisfied spirit.
- *Criticism*—the inclination to backbite, gossip, and feed on the weaknesses of others, due to an uncontrolled tongue.

Need we enlarge such a repulsive catalog? These are not regarded as gross sins; but they are, nevertheless, outworkings of carnality. Is there victory over the flesh? Yes, thank God, this is promised unequivocally in the Word of God. As we shall see later, there is a great secret revealed to us in God's blessed Book whereby the flesh may be kept inoperative through the power of the Holy Spirit, by way of the Cross.

3. *The Devil.* We have thought of the world (that external enemy), and of the flesh (that internal enemy); now we must think of the third great foe—the devil, that infernal enemy! The devil is a person, the actual *prince of the power of the air* (Eph. 2:2). He controls the affairs of *this evil world*, and his great objective is to thwart the divine will and program in the world, in the Church, and in the believer. To this end he presents his challenge along many avenues, and seeks to usurp and dominate the property which, by creative and redemptive claim, rightly belongs to Christ. As a believer, you cannot evade his subtle devices (2 Cor. 2:11). He is your unceasing antagonist (1 Pet. 5:8). He must be met and overcome. Is this possible? Yes, thank God, through the Savior's

victory on the Cross this mighty enemy has been fully and finally vanquished (Heb. 2:14), and one day the whole world shall see the full consummation of this. Meantime, the Evil One is busy in the world, but all his activiites are within the *permissive* will of God. The child of God may have victory in Christ day by day, since the Victorious Christ is an indwelling reality. *Satan to Jesus must bow.* But of this, more later

Do You Believe This?

Now, my reader, are you convinced that the Word promises full victory to every believer? Having known the healing touch of the Good Samaritan upon your sin-wounds, that blessed Benefactor will never leave you to your own resources for the remainder of the journey. Having been delivered from the horrible pit of sin, it never is God's will that you should periodically wander back into its dark domain and stodgy atmosphere. The Savior is more than a guarantor of safety from Hell and sin's penalty. He is sufficiently strong to keep you from sin's dominion day by day (Heb. 7:25). Yes, complete victory is possible all the time, or there must be a defect in the atoning work of Calvary. Since it is proved by abundant Scriptural evidence, as well as in the practical experience of saints of God down through the ages, it remains true to this day. Has Christ changed? Is He not yours? Then such a life is possible for you!

Standing and State

Before closing this chapter, it should be emphasized that the experiential life of Victory deals exclusively with the believer's state day by day, as distinct from his eternal standing in Christ. Every true believer is *in Christ* forever; that is, as to his standing (Phil. 1:1). To *abide* in Christ day by day, however, is a practical matter which concerns his daily walk and conduct (John 15:4). Every believer is indwelled and *sealed with the Holy Spirit* (Eph. 4:30), otherwise he is not a believer (Eph. 1:13). As to his state, however, he is exhorted to *be filled with the Spirit* (Eph. 5:18). Every Christian, in his spiritual standing, possesses life. If his state is to correspond with his *standing,*

19

however, he must learn the secret of life more abundant (John 10:10). Do you see the difference? Your standing in Christ is perfect and complete forever (Heb. 10:14), because the perfect One is the accepted One before God, and you are accepted in Him (Eph. 1:6). The Holy Spirit's function, however, is to make the blessings of our *standing* in Christ *experientially* real day by day, so that others may see Christ in us (1 Pet. 2:9), and that we may be enabled to possess our possessions in Him. Do not allow the devil to confuse your mind over this important, yet simple, distinction. Your standing is what you are IN CHRIST positionally; your state is what you are in practical daily life and conduct. Remember again that the triumphant life is just CHRIST HIMSELF. He is its *Alpha* and *Omega*, the solution of every problem, the answer to every challenge (Rev. 1:8). Since He dwells within you, triumphant Christian life is your spiritual birthright and glorious inheritance. Now, we must consider another important matter which logically arises at this point.

Chapter 2

Who is the Traitor Within?

Inner Conflict

To understand God's way of victory over sin and self, it is vitally important to recognize the flesh vs. Spirit conflict in the believer. Many a young Christian has been bothered about the continued recurrence of former sinful desires. As believers, they have been *born again* and are true children of God; they are as much *justified* before God as ever they will be; yet they are conscious, from time to time, that there is a traitor within who ever challenges the will of God in and through them (Rom. 7:21). With every impulse toward holiness, and every urge of the Holy Spirit towards whole-hearted consecration, there is ever present this other thing which *wars against the soul* (1 Pet. 2:11). The Scripture views him as a child of Adam by natural generation, and as a child of God by spiritual regeneration. When we are born again, we become *partakers of the divine nature* (2 Pet. 1:4). The very nature of Christ Himself is imparted to us by the indwelling Holy Spirit. Since the truest saint, however, is not beyond the range of temptation, or exempt from the possibility of yielding to it, the flesh is obviously still there, and is neither improved nor removed by regeneration.

An Incessant Warfare

This accounts for the fact that the moment you were 'born anew', an incessant warfare commenced in your heart. Paul describes this conflict as: *the flesh lusteth against the Spirit and the Spirit against the flesh* (Gal. 5:17). Each of the two is ever striving for mastery. It is possible for you, as a Christian, to yield to either, and the one to whom you yield, his servant you are (Rom. 6:16). Later, we shall see God's method of victory over this carnal enemy; but, meantime, let us emphasize the fact of its existence. These two are diametrically antagonistic. The flesh *cannot please God* (Rom. 8:8). On the other hand, the divine nature *doth not commit sin* (1 John 3:9). With every impulse of the one, therefore, there is invariably the challenge of the other. Read through Romans 7 and see how the apostle Paul describes his own conflict along this line. *When I would do good*, he says, *evil is present with me* (Rom. 7:21). Now this evil principle of sin has a number of designations in the Scripture. Reference is made to the *law of sin and death* (Rom. 8:2), *the carnal mind* (Rom. 8:7), the *fleshly members*, etc. In the passage quoted already from Galatians, it is enbodied in *the flesh*, and this term we shall use for the purpose of our study. Remember, therefore, that *the flesh* does not refer to this substance that goes to make up our physical bodies, but to the fallen aspect which resides within the body. The term *flesh*, in this sense, is the operative agent of *sin in the flesh* (Romans 8:3), as we shall see later.

The "Self" Life

It has been helpfully suggested that the best way to define *the flesh* is to cross out the 'h' and spell it backwards. This makes SELF and that, after all, is the very essence of the old life. We arrive at this simple conclusion, therefore, that there are two possible centers for every Christian life: SELF or CHRIST. The carnal Christian (1 Cor. 3:3) is one who, though born again, lives a self-centered life and seeks along many avenues (even in Christian work and ministry) to *minister* to self (Rom. 15:3). This produces a desire for praise of self, and possibly, a resentment of anything in the nature of rebuke or correction. This is a sad and subtle temptation, one to which any Christian may yield. We easily become "I" specialists (Luke 18:11,12)! Christendom is infested with a dread malady called "perpendicular-personal-pronoun-I-tis". It is just that big "I", the self life, carnality, intruding into the realm of spiritual experience and service. What a blessed thing to know the way of deliverance from SELF (Rom. 7:25)! Remember, therefore, that the believer possesses these two competitors for the ascendancy, and each is in deadly combat with the other.

Now, it is important that we should see what the Scripture has to say about this traitor within, i.e., the flesh. Let us examine the matter simply and carefully.

1. *Flesh is NOT the physical body.* The Greek word for *body* (*soma*) is quite a different word from that which is used for *the flesh* (*sarx*). The body is a tangible, material substance. *The flesh* is a condition of the soul where we have yielded to indwelling sin. Indeed, the body of every believer was potentially redeemed by the Lord Jesus Christ in His Calvary atonement and actually belongs to God. The term, *vile body* (Phil. 3:21), in our English Authorized Version, is a little misleading. It should read *the body of our humiliation.* The fleshly tabernacle is not something repulsive. It is sacred. It is holy unto the Lord (Rom. 12:1). It is the instrument of righteousness (Rom. 6:13). Every whit should utter His glory (Ps. 29:9). Why, then, is the body referred to as a *body of humiliation*? Because it is the residence of this carnality, and, therefore, is subject to disease, sickness, death, and, oftime, infirmities. The flesh should not be confused with the body. Remember also that the atoning work of Christ included the potential redemption of the body. It will not be actually redeemed (Rom. 8:23), however, until the coming again of the Lord Jesus in the air for His Church. Then this earthly tabernacle, with all its limitations and weaknesses, will give place to a glorified body like unto HIS (Phil. 3:21). In the meantime, the believer is responsible to nurture and care for the body (1 Tim. 4:8), thus keeping it as fit as possible for an earthly instrument of service and a vehicle of divine life. To sin against the body either by neglect or through fleshly indulgences is a sin *against the Lord* (1 Cor. 3:17). Your body belongs to Him; you are only the tenant. It must be presented *a living sacrifice* (Rom. 12:1) to God. To pander to it or use it as an instrument for the mere satisfaction of the flesh, or the exhibition of camouflage beauty, is grieving to the Holy Spirit of God (Gal. 6:12). Real beauty

in the sight of God is not the product of cosmetics but the outshining of the indwelling Christ (Ps. 90:17). A Quaker lady was once asked the secret of her beautiful complexion. She said, "I use truth for my lips; for my voice, prayer; for my eyes, pity; for my hands, charity; for my figure, uprightness; and for my heart, LOVE". These heavenly cosmetics are worthy of trial, and are supplied free to every applicant at the Throne of Grace.

2. *The Flesh is the Residue of the Old Man.* All that a fallen person is by nature is included in God's designation *the flesh* (Col. 3:5,9). Man in his failure and corruption before God is *flesh*. A minister in Scotland was out visiting one day when he called at a house where a "new arrival" had recently blessed the home. The proud mother, carrying the infant in her arms, said to the visitor: "Who do you think he looks like, Doctor?" His reply was, "Very like Adam, Ma'am". That was probably a little disappointment to the mother, but it was sound theology! Yes, all that we are by virtue of our natural generation is flesh—but more about this in a later chapter.

3. *Flesh, therefore, is operative when we yield to indwelling sin.* There are some who do not distinguish *flesh* from *indwelling sin.* This invariably leads to confusion and error. The apostle Paul gives a very ugly and replusive catalog of sins in Galatians 5:19, to which even a Christian may yield if he fails to live under the domination of his new nature. Where do these ugly things come from? The apostle is careful to tell us that they are the *works of the flesh.* Who could doubt, therefore, that the flesh embraces *indwelling sin*? Paul again refers, in another connection, to *sin in the flesh* (Rom. 8:3). Everything that displeased God finds its birth in *the flesh.* Some may argue that the Scriptures quoted have sole reference to *the natural* [unsaved] *man.* This is not so, however, for similar warnings concerning the *sins of the flesh* (Eph. 5:18) are included in the Epistles to the Church, and in close proximity to the highest doctrines of spiritual experience. Truly, the believer must ever walk close to the Lord, and appropriate the divine means of victory if he is to know deliv-

erance from the subtle maneuverings of this traitor within. In Romans 7:22, the new man in Christ had no will to violate God's purpose. It is *sin that dwelleth* in him.

4. *The flesh cannot be eradicated or annihilated.* This is very important, and this paragraph should be read in conjunction with the special chapter later devoted to the consideration, "Is it sinless perfection?". Little more need be said on this point here. In Romans 7, Paul expressly declared: "I am carnal". As you know, there are three classes of men spoken of in the Epistles:

   · *The Natural Man*—the unregenerate child of Adam (1 Cor. 2:14).
   · *The Carnal Man*—the 'born again' believer living under the domination of *the flesh* (Rom. 7:14).
   · *The Spiritual Man*—the believer who is *filled with the Spirit* (1 Cor. 2:15).

   Of whom is the apostle speaking in Romans 7? Of himself as *carnal*. Therefore, he recognizes the presence of *the flesh* within. In fact, he actually speaks of himself as in captivity to this fleshly nature. When he *would do good, evil is present*. With every desire of holiness, he is conscious of another law operating in his members. What is this law but the law of sin (Rom. 7:25)? He further says, "Let not sin therefore reign in your mortal bodies". This clearly implies that sin is present, but it must not be allowed to prevail. It cannot, therefore, be eradicated.

   I once met a dear Christain who appeared to advocate the annihilation theory in his ministry. I asked him why he emphasized eradication. His reply was that he did not teach eradication, but used an even stronger word, the word which God used. "Oh," I said, "what is that?" He said "destroyed", and then quoted Romans 6:6. "Well," I responded, "tell me, is the devil destroyed in _____?" mentioning the name of his home town. He admitted that this was far from being true. I then pointed out that Hebrews 2:14 clearly pronounces that the devil is *destroyed*, the same word as is used in Romans 6:6. It is obvious, therefore, that the force of the word is not annihilated or abolished, but rather, *rendered inoperative*, or *put out of action*, or *made of none effect*. This is a very different significance. The devil is very busy today, in this age (Luke 22:53), and a worse climax will even yet be reached as the age draws on to its midnight (Rom. 13:12). Yet, the devil is a defeated foe (Col. 2:15). He was vanquished through the death of the Lord Jesus, and the believer may know constant victory over him through the greater power of the indwelling Christ (1 John 4:4). I trust this distinction is clear. *The Son of God was manifested that He might destroy the works of the devil* (1 John 3:8). This he actually accomplished nearly two millennia ago, though the full consummation of His work is not yet apparent. That is yet to be. In the same way, *the flesh* is not desroyed in the sense of obliteration, but, thank God, it has been *crucified* (Gal. 5:24) and may be mortified, as we shall see in a later chapter. Another important fact to recognize is that:

5. *The flesh includes not only gross sin, but all humanistic natural goodness.* This is vitally imporant truth, but often unrecognized. If *the flesh* includes all that a person is naturally, it obviously embraces the good and attractive side of human nature. Yes, *the flesh* has a good side. The natural man may, and often does, possess very delightful qualities (Matt. 19:16-22). He may be kind, amiable, generous, gracious, artistic, religious, well-inclined, accomplished—and possess many other admirable virtues from a human standpoint. It must be remembered, however, that *human goodness is never spiritual* (Rom. 3:12). *There is none that doeth good; no, not one* (Ps. 14:3). The flesh does not contain, and cannot produce, anything spiritual. *I know that in me, that is, in my flesh, dwelleth no good thing* (Rom. 7:18). They that are in the flesh cannot please God (Rom. 8:8). Our blessed Lord also said, *The flesh profiteth nothing* (John 6:63). The two vital words which God writes over the flesh are CANNOT and NOTHING. It is utterly futile, therefore, to try and improve or patch up the flesh. God can never accept it. It is utterly beyond any hope of recovery. God has *condemned* it, root, branch, and fruit (Rom. 8:3). There is ever a subtle

danger of Christians investing in shares and interests in "The Old Adam Improvement Society". It is an utterly bankrupt concern, however. The Holy Spirit describes it in commercial phraseology. It is *no good* and *profiteth nothing.* It pays no spiritual dividends. God can never recognize *flesh,* however humanly attractive it may be.

The fact that it includes human goodness is clearly stressed in the apostle Paul's own testimony—

> *For we are the circumcision, which worship God in the spirit, and rejoice in Christ Jesus, and have no confidence in the flesh. Though I might also have confidence in the flesh. If any other man thinketh that he hath whereof he might trust in the flesh, I more: Circumcised the eighth day, of the stock of Israel, of the tribe of Benjamin, an Hebrew of the Hebrews; as touching the law, a Pharisee; Concerning zeal, persecuting the church; touching the righteousness which is in the law, blameless. But what things were gain to me, those I counted loss for Christ* (Phil. 3:3-7).

Yes, the apostle was a good, honest, sincere religionist before his conversion. Which of us could submit such a claim as, *I have lived in all good conscience before God until this day* (Acts 23:1)? Here was a good, religious, moral enthusiast on the road to Hell. He was not an adulterer, or a thief, or a murderer. His morality and his religion were scrupulous. Yet it all belonged to *the flesh.*

So also was Nicodemus (John 3). Here was a conscientious devotee of the law; he was a master in Israel. All his good qualities, however, could never be recognized by God because they belonged to the natural man. He must receive a new life. We can now understand why even good people need to be 'born again'. God places a vital line of demarcation between *flesh* and *Spirit.* The one is death and the other is life. The *natural man* is dead in trespasses and sins. He needs to be spiritually quickened. Our blessed Lord emphasized a logical principle when He stated, *That which is born of the flesh is flesh* (John 3:6). Of course it is. It can never become anything else. It may go to Church and be religious, but that is *religious* flesh. It may be accomplished, but it is only *accomplished* flesh. You may try to educate a baby pig, but it *remains* a pig, and all your attempts to improve the manners or appearance of the little creature do not change its nature (Jer. 13:23). At the first opportunity it will reveal this fact by scampering off again to the dirty pigsty.

The human can never develop into the spiritual. All that man is by nature, therefore, is *flesh*—good and bad. He may possess wonderful talents by the endowment of natural inheritance, or by human genius, but even these are unacceptable to God until they are lifted into the realm of the Spirit and become animated by divine life. The flesh ever *serves the law of sin* (Rom. 7:25). From the divine standpoint, it can never make any contribution to the heavenly program. Now it is also important to remember, particularly in relation to the life of victory, that *the flesh* in the believer is *exactly the same* as in the unbeliever. That accounts for the sad fact that if a believer loses touch with the Lord, he may backslide into sins which would hardly be named among decent living men of high moral standards (Rom. 6:21). As we have seen already, the difference between the saved and the unsaved man is that the former has a new nature—a divine nature. Notice also, that:

6. *The flesh possesses a will of its own.* John 1:13 speaks of *the will of the flesh*, i.e., the natural or fleshly will. The spiritual man says, *Not my will, but Thine, be done* (Luke 22:42). He is not governed by his personal likes or dislikes. The yielding to the will of the flesh necessarily involves an arrest of spiritual life. A Christian may yield to the impulses of a fleshly will, producing carnal decisions and natural judgments (John 8:15), even in relation to spiritual problems. This must result in confusion and consequent grieving of the Holy Spirit (Eph. 4:30). The Lord is never glorified through a decision of the flesh, even though it comes within the circle of orthodox service. The flesh possesses a zeal of its own, but such zeal is *not according to knowledge* (Rom. 10:2).

Beware of responding to any call or deciding upon any course of action at the impulse of the natural will. Pray before you act and be sure you hear *What the Spirit saith* (Rev 2;7). The new man in Christ hears a voice behind him saying *This is the Way, walk you in it* (Is 30;21). What havoc and desolation have been wrought in many a redeemed life and many an assembly because of an important judgment arrived at in the flesh! Further, how often a fleshly judgment has manifested itself in the imputation of a wrong motive and a harsh, unkind conclusion concerning another Christian. *The flesh* is responsible for all unjust criticism; it has a language of its own. The fleshly tongue is set on fire of hell (James 3:6). There is a spiritual and constructive criticism which redounds to the Lord's glory. Let us see to it that before we speak critically of another we ask the Lord to put the purification of the Cross upon our fleshly lips, and first question ourselves along this line: "Is it true? Is it kind? Is it necessary?" Notice lastly:

7. *The flesh has its lusts* (Rom. 13:14; Gal. 5:24; Eph. 2:3; 1 Pet. 2:11; 2 Pet. 2:18). Look up the Scriptures in these references, and see what God has to say about this matter. The *lusts of the flesh* can only be conquered by a *walk in the Spirit* (Gal. 5:16), and a definite refusal to make any provision for their fulfillment. A boy was told by his mother that he was not to bathe in certain water, and if ever he were tempted to do so, he was to refuse the suggestion of the Evil One. One day he disobeyed; and when asked why he had done so, he said that the devil tempted him, and he could not resist. His mother saw that he had returned with his bathing suit, however, and at once asked the boy why he had taken his togs with him. Said the boy, "I took them *in case I might be tempted*". Moral: *Make no provision for the lusts of the flesh.*

So much, then, for *the flesh.* What a repulsive thing it is in the sight of God! What should be the Christian's attitude toward this evil factory of sin and unrighteousness? We should hate it (Jude 23). We shall see how it can be overcome. The victorious life is not trying to conquer SINS, as some seem to

The New Life

believe. What a hopeless and disappointing task that is! Real victory finds deliverance from the power of indwelling SIN.

A Christian often used to pray at his prayer meeting— "Lord, take away the cobwebs of sin from my life". The poor man was evidently fighting his sins one by one, and seemed to be enveloped in carnal cobwebs! Another saint was present, however, who knew more about the divine way of victory, and he got to his feet and prayed, "Lord, kill THE SPIDER!"

Now in the next chapter we shall see the divine method of dealing with *the flesh*, this internal traitor!

Chapter 3

What is the Deeper Meaning of the Cross?

Identification with Christ

Do you realize, my brother or sister, that there is a deeper meaning of the Cross, constituting a much neglected and vitally important aspect of the atoning work of the Lord Jesus Christ on Calvary? While the substitutionary work of the Savior is the only ground of a sinner's justification, it is important to realize that the Atonement embraces something more even than that. The Savior's redemptive work also includes the glorious fact of *Identification.* This we must consider under the careful illumination and guidance of the Holy Spirit in order to apprehend the divine way of victory. If there is one subject more than another which arouses the antipathy of the Evil One, and about which he uses every endeavor to keep God's people in darkness, it is this second and deeper aspect of the Atonement. Let us pray as we consider it.

We have seen that *the flesh* dwells within these bodies of humiliation, and will so remain until the early course is completed. In Old Testament typology, Amalek (Ex. 17:8) represents the flesh. You will remember that war is declared upon him *from generation to generation* (Ex. 17:16) until *finally* his remembrance is *put out* forever (Ex. 17:14). This cannot be until we have glorified bodies, liberated from the very *presence* of sin. In the meantime, how can this corruption be dealt with? That is the problem to which many an earnest Christian is seeking a genuine solution.

Is it God's decree that this evil root of sin should continually bring forth its poisonous fruit, leaving the Christian to pluck off the berries one by one as they appear? Must the spider be allowed to envelop the life with its wretched cobwebs? Has the believer no alternative but a recurring experience of sinning and repenting?

Yes, thank God, there is a more excellent way. Here is good news. Follow this carefully. In the glorious pupose of redemption, the flesh *has already been dealt with fully and finally at the Cross of Calvary.* In the expiatory sacrifice of Christ, not only were sins righteously atoned for, but SIN (in its entirety) was *PUT AWAY* (Heb. 9:26). Calvary penetrates to the very heart of the question, and in the death of the Lord Jesus, *God saw the end of the old Adam life, the corrupt fallen human nature, and wound it up forever as an utterly bankrupt concern.* In other words, every believer was represented and incorporated into the death of the Lord Jesus. *He died unto sin once* (Rom. 6:10), and therefore every believer, in the purpose of God, *died with Him.* The Cross marks the death–knell and the complete termination of *the flesh* in the sight of God. I want to quote you a few references on this important matter:

> *What shall we say then? Shall we continue in sin, that grace may abound? God forbid. How shall we, that are dead to sin, live any longer therein? Know ye not, that so many of us as were baptized into Jesus Christ were baptized into his death? Therefore we are buried with him by baptism into death: that like as Christ was raised up from the dead by the glory of the Father, even so we also should walk in newness of life. For if we have been planted together in the likeness of his death, we shall be also in the likeness of his resurrection: Knowing this, that our old man is crucified with him, that the body of sin might be destroyed, that henceforth we should not serve sin. For he that is dead is freed from sin. Now if we be dead with Christ, we believe that we shall also live with him:* (Rom. 6:1-8)

*For what the law could not do, in that it was weak
through the flesh, God sending His own Son in the
likeness of sinful flesh, and for sin, condemned
sin in the flesh (Rom. 8:3).*

*For the love of Christ constraineth us; because we
thus judge, that if one died for all, then were all
dead (2 Cor. 5:14).*

*That I may know Him, and the power of His resur-
rection, and the fellowship of his sufferings, being
made conformable unto his death (Phil. 3:10).*

*For ye are dead, and your life is hid with Christ
in God (Col. 3:3).*

What has God done, therefore, with the flesh? He does
not *forgive* it or *condone* it. God forgives *the sinner* but He
condemns sin (Matt. 6:14,15). Do you see, therefore, that in the
Savior's representative capacity, God saw the death of every believer at the Cross, as far as the flesh–life is concerned? "If One
died for all, *then all have died.*"

All Have Died

He dealt with the whole sin question as your *Representative* and mine. A representative is one who acts *on behalf* of
another. An ambassador's actions and words are those of the
country he represents. The Lord Jesus *died unto sin* as your
Representative. So far as your self-life is concerned, therefore,
your existence came to an end nearly two thousand years ago
in the divine purpose. It may be you do not understand that.
Never mind—believe it! God says so. *"Our old man has been
crucified with Him."*

I have read a story which may make this clear to you. During the American Civil War, when men were drawn by lot to
join the Army, a man named Wyatt was called up to fight for
the South. He was the breadwinner for his family, and they
were entirely dependent upon him. Realizing this hardship,
another young man named Pratt volunteered to go instead. He

was accepted and drafted to the Front *bearing the name and number of Wyatt.* Eventually, Pratt was killed in action, and having died as the substitute and in the name of the other man, the full name of Wyatt was recorded killed in action. At a later date, Wyatt was again called up for service; but at the Recruiting Office, he calmly stated that *he had already been killed in action.* The entry was searched for and discovered, and Wyatt, although alive and well, was dead *in the eyes of the authorities* because he was identified with his substitute. Does that help you to understand it?

You *died* with Him. You were *buried* with Him. You were *planted together* in the likeness of His death. You were *crucified* with Him. All this is an accomplished fact in the heavenly purpose, apart altogether from the believer's apprehension of it. The way by which it is made real in experience is another matter which we will deal with in the next chapter. Meantime, lay hold of the fact that God has conclusively dealt with the flesh nearly two millenia ago in the death of His Son.

Having seen this, another blessed fact is also revealed, that every believer has also been *identified with Him in His resurrection and His ascension.* Read the following passages:

> *Therefore we are buried with him by baptism into death: that like as Christ was raised up from the dead by the glory of the Father, even so we also should walk in newness of life. For if we have been planted together in the likeness of his death, we shall be also in the likeness of his resurrection* (Rom. 6:4,5).

> *Now if we be dead with Christ, we believe that we shall also live with him: Knowing that Christ being raised from the dead dieth no more; death hath no more dominion over him* (Rom. 6:8,9).

> *But God, who is rich in mercy, for his great love wherewith he loved us, Even when we were dead in sins, hath quickened us* [made us alive] *together with Christ, (by grace ye are saved); And hath raised us up together, and made us sit together in*

*heavenly places in Christ Jesus: That in the ages
to come he might shew the exceeding riches of his
grace in his kindness toward us through Christ
Jesus (Eph. 2:4-7).*

Dead, Buried, Raised, and Ascended with Him

Now let us examine the mighty sweep of this tremendous
truth. Every believer without exception, every member of the
Body of Christ, every justified sinner, is seen by God as one
with Christ in His death, burial, resurrection, and ascension
(1 Cor. 6:17). We, thus, conclude that three mighty transactions
were effected at Calvary.

Three Calvary Facts

1. The believer's sins were righteously forgiven.

2. The flesh, that internal traitor, was condemned and put
   away. [Its authority was cancelled.]

3. The birth of a *new creation* took place. A New Man in con-
   trast to *the Old Man* came into being, and every believer
   forms an integral part of that new creation, *joined to the
   Lord one Spirit.* To what intent? That he should no longer
   live unto himself (i.e., to *the flesh*) but henceforth *unto Him
   which died for them and rose again* (2 Cor. 5:15).

All this is a blessed accomplishment in the divine purpose,
to find practical outworking in experience day by day. Look
again at Romans 6. In verse 4, the objective is *newness of life.*
That means that the believer should possess a new mind, a new
heart, new desires, new ambitions, new pursuits, new joys, a
new peace, a new power, a new victory—in fact, *all things are
become new* (2 Cor. 5:17). *The flesh* (Col. 3:9) ceases its dominion. The believer is no longer debtor to the flesh (Rom. 8:12),
i.e., no longer under any obligation to serve sin, any more than
the children of Israel were under further obligation to Pharaoh
as they marched out of his dominion in that victorious passage
through the Red Sea.

Do you appreciate, my reader, that the Cross means something more than the Lord Jesus dying for our sins? Take that second look at the Cross and ask God to reveal its meaning to your heart:

> *I have been crucified with Christ, nevertheless I live, yet not I, but Christ liveth in me* (Gal. 2:20).

> *Ye died, and your life is hid with Christ in God* (Col. 3:3).

Believest thou this?

The Fact and the Experience of It

The next question that arises quite logically and normally in the mind is that experience often indicates that the flesh in the believer's life is NOT eradicated. It is often very much alive and manifests itself in distressing ways which mar his testimony, disturb his joy, and hinder his usefulness. How can this apparent contradiction be reconciled? The Word of God clearly declares that *the old man* is crucified, whereas experience proves beyond doubt that *the flesh* often asserts itself like a jack-in-the-box at the least provocation, and at the most unexpected moments!

Now, we need to recognize the distinction between what happened *once and for all* in the eternal purpose at the Cross (Eph. 3:11), and that which is made true *in experience* day by day. Obviously, there may be a vital difference. While it stands eternally true that a full and complete salvation was wrought out to its finality at the Cross, its blessings do not become practically real in exprience *until they are appropriated.* How may this be done? The answer is simple. BY FAITH (Heb. 11:1).

Think of your conversion for a moment. Was it not true and an accomplished fact that Jesus died for you long before you experienced this benefit? Why, certainly; before your conversion it was *just as true* as after your conversion. What made the difference then? *You believed it* and accepted Him into your heart, did you not? How did you receive Him? By faith (Eph. 2:8). So that faith made God's eternal fact of value to you personally. Do you see that? Let us pursue this important enquiry in the next chapter.

.

The New Life

Chapter 4

How Does Calvary Become Real in the Believer's Life?

The Art of Reckoning

Here we come to the blessed theme of the triumphant *reckoning* of faith. Turn to Romans 6 again. What do we find the apostle exhorting in verse 11? His logic is perfect. Having emphasized the believer's death with Christ, he now says:

> *Likewise reckon ye also yourselves to be dead indeed unto sin* (Rom. 6:11).

Reckon on what? Reckon on God's fact that *the old man has been crucified* with Christ, and that you have been raised again with Him into *newness of life*. The *fact*, of course, is eternal. Even my unbelief does not alter the truth of God, though it will rob me of the blessing of it (Rom. 3:3).

What does it mean to reckon? Surely it is simply counting on a fact. I am told that a pool of ice is strong enough to bear me. Immediately I stand upon the ice, however, and commit myself to it, I reckon on the fact and actually prove it true. A sum of money is credited to my account in the bank. Even though it is mine, it may long remain unenjoyed and unappropriated. Immediately I draw my check, however, when I present it at the bank for payment I reckon on the fact that the money belongs to me and actually possess my possessions.

Victory...Even Our Faith

Now this is tremendously important. The Christian life, from its Alpha to its Omega, is essentially a life of faith.

This is the victory...even our faith (1 John 5:4).

What does real faith accomplish? It turns God's promises into facts of experience (Heb. 6:12). No potential blessing in Christ becomes real to me until it is appropriated, and that by the victorious act of reckoning. A condemned prisoner may be offered a signed pardon, but it is only a scrap of paper until it is appropriated. It is his, potentially, immediately it is signed, but it is not his experientially until he claims it and acts upon it.

Now how does this work out in the Christian's experience? Very simply and very blessedly, God says in effect, "my child, as you reckoned on the substitutionary work of the Lord Jesus Christ for your salvation, now go a step further and reckon on His representative work for your victory day by day". You believe that the Lord Jesus died for you because God said so. Now take the next step. Accept by faith the further fact that *you died with Him*, i.e., that your *old man was crucified with Him*. Believe also that you rose with Him into newness of life, and, henceforth, *reckon yourself to be dead indeed unto sin, but alive unto God.* Do you see that, my fellow believer? If so, you will appreciate at once that victory (1 Cor. 15:57) does not come by struggling or agonizing, but by reckoning (2 Cor. 4:10).

Come Down From the Cross

Let me suggest a further practical consideration along this line. What will happen if you *reckon yourself dead to sin?* Imagine the devil approaching you, as he doubtless does, with temptation to sin (James 1:13). What part of you can respond to him? Obviously not *the new man*, for, *that which is born of God doth not commit sin.* Any response, therefore, will come from *the flesh.* Exactly. The devil's objective is to get the flesh into activity, for the flesh is the devil's battleground. Yes, the Savior's temptation is that of everyone who is joined to him: *Come down from the Cross* (Matt. 27:40). Thank God; He won the victory in that supreme hour and became obedient unto death (Phil 2:8).

You and I also may share His triumph by reckoning on the fact that we are identified with Him. Suppose, then, that in this moment of temptation you assume a simple attitude of faith and *reckon yourself to be dead to sin*; what is the result? We read, *He that hath died is freed from sin* (Rom. 6:7). Testify to the evil one that you are dead: "No, these hands cannot commit sin because they have been crucified with Christ". Tell me, what can the devil do with dead hands? Do you see? "This is the victory...even our faith." Wherever or whatever the temptation may be, therefore, there is a way of escape (1 Cor. 10:13).

Dying—Not Doing

A dead man cannot respond to sinful inducements, however alluring. Imagine a man, addicted to alcohol, drinking himself to death. There is his lifeless corpse! Now you may surround his body with all the strong drink you can discover. What is the effect? NIL! For what reason? Drink has exercised its full dominion over him. He is now dead, and there is no further response. Apply the illustration. Death exercised its full dominion over the Lord Jesus as He was made sin for you and me. You and I have been incorporated into His death. Therefore, argues the apostle, *sin shall not have dominion over you* (Rom 6:14). Is not that the victory you have been seeking? We can only conquer sin and self by picking up our Cross daily.

I have heard of two society girls who were gloriously converted to God. A few days after they were saved, an invitation came from some of their former friends to attend the theatre. They had no further desire for the things of the world, however; and their reply was both courteous and interesting. It was to this effect: "Thank you for your kind invitation to go to the theatre; we cannot attend, however, as we are dead! We died with Christ a week ago." That is it!

Now it is clear that victory comes through the reckoning of faith and not through struggling and striving. "But", it may be asked, "are we not exhorted to *fight the good fight*" (1 Tim. 6:12)? Yes, that is so; but you must please finish the text: *Fight the good fight OF FAITH*, and faith never struggles for victory.

Faith stands IN victory, and combats the forces of darkness from a victory position.

Standing in Victory

Yes, the Christian does not fight for victory but stands IN a victory already won. But are not Christians exhorted to resist the devil (James 4:7)? Certainly; but here again please remember the other word, *Whom resist, steadfast in the faith* (1 Pet. 5:9). You see it is faith holding a position, and not struggling for a position. What a blessed secret is here revealed! Reckon! Reckon! Reckon! Rest on God's FACT.

I heard of a Christian who asked another to pray for him, particularly that he 'might be *nothing*'. "There is no need to pray for that, brother", answered the other, "you ARE nothing; *accept it by faith.*"

Apply this death-principle to all fleshly manifestations. Are you tempted to jealousy? Then reckon yourself to be dead. Can a dead man be jealous? Are you subject to the tyranny of a hasty tongue? Does the unkind word slip out? Reckon yourself to be *crucified with Christ.* Can a crucified man say unkind things? Are you sensitive to the opinions, the criticism, or the eulogies of others? Reckon yourself dead. Can a dead man be offended? Go to a cemetery; find the grave of a man you knew; make a trumpet with both your hands, and shout over that grave all the praise or blame, eulogy or hatred, of which you are capable, and you only waste your time! He is dead, and quite impervious to other people's opinions. Simple enough, yes, but that is the way of victory. God's way is simple.

Dead Men Canot Sin

Who is blind, but My servant? Or deaf, as My messenger that I send? Who is blind as he that is at peace with Me, and blind as the Lord's servant? Thou seest many things, but thou observest not; his ears are open, but he heareth not (Is. 42:19,20).

The servant of God may see, and yet be blind; he may hear, and yet be deaf. He may have lips, and yet be silent. He may be dead, and yet live.

> I am not now what once I was,
> Nor am I what I ought to be,
> But what I am, I am by grace
> And when I see Him face to face,
> I shall be like Him perfectly.
> I once was dead, yet thought I lived,
> And now I live, yet dead I am—
> I live in Him with whom I died,
> My life, my song, is Calvary's Lamb.

A Christian man recently wrote, concerning his relation to a certain important work in connection with which one of his suggestions had not been acted upon, "I just want to keep a humble out-of-sight place in my relation to that work, and be everything else. I am nothing, anyway, and I don't want anyone ever to succeed in making me think that I am anything; for if they do, from that time on I'll be nothing in the worst sort of sense. So just feel free to write me anything that is on your heart, critical or otherwise, and ask God to give me grace to take it in the way that a WISE DEAD man ought to take it. I am His bondslave." Yes, we can be dead, and we can be wise at the same time. Indeed, until we have accepted our own death through crucifixion with Christ, we can never let the wisdom of God have free course in our life.

But Alive Unto God

Then, remember the other side and reckon also on the fact that you have been raised together with Christ. *I have been crucified with Christ, nevertheless I live, yet not I, but Christ liveth in me* (Gal 2:20). Do you see that? Your whole being has come under a new control. "This business is under new management." While it is true, therefore, that we are to be dead to sin, we are not to be corpses. VICTORY IS LIFE. Having been identified with Him, in His risen life, these same members, this identical body, this very mind and intellect, these same faculties—reckoned dead to sin—are now to be alive unto God. Your whole being is to come under the domination of the new nature which is energized by the Christ-life. When the devil knocks at the door with his seductive suggestions, he is told to go his way, for the old and loyal friend (the *old man*) who used to welcome him has now ceased to exist. Such an attitude alone can overcome his subtle devices. Yes, Calvary is Victory.

Then, there comes another appeal! Here is a request, or urge, from the Holy Spirit to some service for the kingdom of God. What is your response now? "Yes, Lord, here am I; here are my hands, my feet, my mind, my time, my money; they are all Thine, Lord, and I am ready for Thy commands. Take me, use me, fill me, and keep me ever responsive to Thy will. I am not my own, I am bought with a price." You see it is simply saying "no" to the devil, and "yes" to the Lord, i.e., dead unto sin but alive unto God. Victory is yours, therefore, by Calvary becoming experientially real in your life day by day.

Nearly two thousand years ago the devil was overthrown; the world was overcome, and the *old man* was crucified at Calvary (Gal. 2:20, c.f. Rom. 6:11). There the *Seed of the woman* (Gen. 3:15) bruised the serpent's head; there the evil one was ignominiously defeated on his own battleground. Calvary, blest Calvary! Only as Calvary is worked out in the believer day by day, by a consent to the *sentence of death* (2 Cor. 1:9) upon *the old life*, and a recognition of the claims of Him with whom we have risen into newness of life, can we discover victory in practical experience.

Now two further points concerning the reckoning of faith need to be emphasized here:

It is Not a "Once For All" Reckoning

Reckoning ourselves as dead indeed unto sin is not a *final crisis*, but a *continuous process*. It is not a second blessing (nor is it a millionth blessing, for that matter). It represents blessings innumerable every day. The Christian life is essentially a *moment-by-moment* life. It is a continuous dying, and a continuous living. Of course, there may come a particular crisis in experience where the Spirit of God brings the soul face to face with a definite issue as to a *willingness* for the Cross, and full surrender of the whole life to God. Yes, the first revelation of the secret of victory also may constitute a real crisis in the life of the believer, but *that crisis or experience can never, in itself, avail for the future.*

There is a subtle danger in relying upon some isolated experience of *sanctification* so called. The victorious Christian life is a Person, not an experience. Following the crisis, whatever phase or landmark in the life that may represent, there must be the daily reckoning, the moment-by-moment abiding, and the unceasing control of the Holy Spirit. *Always bearing about in the body the dying of the Lord Jesus* (2 Cor. 4:10). Whatever may have been your experience of holiness and the measure of spiritual attainments in the past, y*ou can never get beyond the need for abiding in Christ* (1 John 2:28) *and the continuous reckoning of faith.* Fail to reckon and *the flesh* is at once resurrected!

In other words, to forfeit the faith position is to offer capital to the enemy (Eph. 4:27) and a battleground upon which he may pursue his challenge. Unmortified flesh is the devil's hunting ground. The Christian life, therefore, is one continuous impartation of life from above, by the indwelling Holy Spirit, made possible by the continuous dethronement of the self-life.

Beware of depending upon externalities for the subsistence of your Christian life. God has graciously given to His people means of grace which indispensably contribute to the outworking of His purpose, but these agencies must never be depended upon in themselves, or allowed to be substitutes for a moment-by-moment intercourse with the Lord Jesus. He is your life, not *things* (Col. 3:4)! Some of God's dear people are *Conference Christians,* for example. They almost live on conferences; they seem to attend every meeting with scrupulous regularity, and by the end of a particular series of meetings, with its fresh impetus, they are *charged up* like an electric battery, and go their way again in the wistful hope that they will hold out until the advent of the next conference! Beloved, that is not God's way. Thank God for conferences, with their spiritual ministry and delightful Christian fellowship. They are undoubtedly divine appointments and means of grace and strengthening to the Church. Never allow them, however, to become the basis of your spiritual experience. Nothing can substitute for a constant, personal moment-by-moment communion with the Most

High. Indeed, one of the real tests of the victorious life is an ability to go on with the Lord in constant, joyous victory, even though there may be an unavoidable severance from conferences and the fellowship of other believers. The Word of God declares that two may put ten thousand to flight (Deut. 32:30, Josh. 23:10). The two are the believer and his Lord!

Now the other thing that needs to be said in this connnection is:

Reckoning is Not a Mere Mental Effort

It is a mental reckoning, of course, but not solely a process of the mind. Some young Christians have been bothered because they have *tried hard to reckon themselves dead to sin*, but somehow it did not work. Why is this? The main reason is that God always links *reckoning* with *surrender*. In Romans 6, these injunctions are associated (Rom. 6:11,13). To attempt to reckon yourself dead to sin without yielding your will to the Holy Spirit will inevitably lead to failure and discouragement. A mental reckoning, in itself, can never sustain victory. *The 'old man' can only be reckoned dead by the power of the new life.* Such power is imparted by the Holy Spirit when the whole being—spirit, soul, and body—is surrendered to Him (Rom. 8:13)

If your will is unyielded all your reckoning will be futile. Your will must be handed over to the Lord and be energized by divine power (John 5:30). Only as you are occupied with Christ in the power of an ungrieved Spirit, can you successfully *reckon* on death to sin. *The flesh cannot mortify the flesh*; the indwelling Spirit alone can impart the power to do so. The blessed function of the Holy Spirit is to make the LIFE of the Lord Jesus real in the believer day by day. That is a liberating life. The gateway into resurrection-life is by way of death, and the way to die is to yield to the new life. The two are inseparable.

Pardon a personal allusion just here. For years I was a cigarette smoker, though a Christian. One day the Lord spoke clearly to me in conviction about this habit. I wanted to be free, but I knew very well that so long as my will was unyielded, and the *want to* was there, all my reckoning would end in failure! The supreme need was to LET GO and y*ield my members to the Lord* for His supreme control. By His grace I consented so to do, and at once there was a blessed accession of divine life and a loss of appetite for the weed. Praise His Name, since then I have possessed the *spiritual ability* to reckon *that dead men do not smoke!* This side of reckoning is vastly important. Only as you *yield*, can you reckon. *Ye through the SPIRIT do mortify...*

BUT IF IT DIE

Now, it is manifest that the Holy Spirit will bring the believer face to face with a definite issue along this line. Am I prepared to say Amen to a real outworking of the Cross? It is not sufficient to give assent to this truth as a matter of objective doctrine. Indeed, it is sadly possible to have a very *high doctrine* and *very low practice.* The real issue is this: Am I willing to die? This is an experiential death, a real death. *Except a corn of wheat fall into the ground and die, it abideth alone, BUT IF IT DIE it bringeth forth much fruit* (John 12:24). Of course, this has primary reference to the Lord Jesus, but it is essentially the way of blessing for all His followers.

I was impressed some time ago by the words which preceded the divine description of those seven downward steps of the Lord Jesus from the Glory to the Cross in Philippians 2. You will recollect that the climax is His *obedience unto death, even the death of the Cross.* Notice the preceding sentence: *Let this mind be IN YOU, which was also in Christ Jesus* (Phil. 2:5). Yes, have I the mind of Christ to this same end (1 Cor. 2:16)? Am I willing, for example, that my reputation should go to Calvary (Phil. 2:7)? Am I willing to *humble myself* and become *obedient unto death* (Phil. 2:8)? Nothing short of this is involved in the Lord's appeal. Until the cross means this to you and me, it means little. *If any man will follow Me, let him deny himself and take up HIS CROSS and follow Me* (Matt. 16:24).

What is the cross, after all? It is not a fetish, or an object to be admired, or a charm to be hung around the neck. No, indeed! There is only one cross, and *that is the cross of the Lord Jesus Christ,* essentially a symbol of death. It is *something to die on.* To take up my cross is to consent to a sentence of death upon myself. Self-denial is not forfeiting a few luxuries during a certain period, and then returning to their indulgence again with a sigh of relief when the Lenten era has expired! No, *self-denial* is not a forfeiting of things, but the abandonment, the dethronement, the abnegation and crucifixion of SELF. The cross is the big "I" cross out!

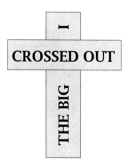

As Dr. E. J. Pace suggests in one of his cartoons, Christian means CHRIST and the I-A-N stands for I AM NOTHING (John 3:30). Here we come to the crux of the whole matter concerning personal victory and an effective, holy, happy Christian testimony. There can be no Crown without the Cross. There can be no life without death. There can be no *Canaan* without *Jordan.*

The Eternal Fact

Let us not think of the Cross as an isolated event in the history of the universe. It is a great eternal fact in the purpose of God. It was no afterthought, or merely an unhappy termination to a wonderful life. It is not a postscript of God's letter to men. Way back in eternity past there was *The Lamb slain from the foundation of the world* (Rev. 13:8). Look into eternity future and see the redeemed multitudes surrounding the throne of God and of the *Lamb as it has been* (freshly) *slain* (Rev. 5:6). Calvary lies between the two eternities, and during this interim the purpose of the Holy Spirit is to work out the meaning of the Cross in the Church and in the individual believer, thus enabling the Body to function effectively in the life of the risen Head. No flesh can intrude in this sphere (1 Cor. 1:29). It must die.

The Real Issue

My brother, my sister, before we pass on to a more definite consideration of the risen life of the Lord Jesus in the believer, shall we, you and I together, face this question? Am I, are you, willing to die? Are we prepared for the Holy Spirit to plant the Cross upon our flesh-life? Shall we say *yes* to the nails of the Cross going through those ugly things which have marred our testimony and over which we have never gained victory? Shall we tell the Lord that we are willing for Jordan as the only way into the promised land of Canaan? This means the burial in the waters (Josh. 4:9) of death of the stones of the self-life. Twelve other stones were taken from the bed of the river and placed on Canaan's soil (Josh. 4:8); a beautiful picture of resurrection-life out from the waters of death. The word comes in freshness to writer and reader alike today, *GO OVER THIS JORDAN* (Josh. 1:2).

The power of God makes this possible as we go through with Him. There is no other way. Nature itself illustrates this abiding principle in all the works of God. *All life is born out of death.* The autumn leaves fall to their death, by the power of, and in order to make way for the advent of, new life; and notice how God paints them with special tints—red and gold, the red to remind us of the Cross, whilst the gold speaks of the Glory. How often the sufferings of Christ are linked with His glory (1 Pet. 1:11)!

His way is your way, dear Christian. Watch that magnificent sunset at the close of a calm, summer day. See that exquisite glory which illuminates the heavens. That *greater light* gives forth its most exquisite radiance *after it has sunk* below the horizon. Yes, there is a glory in the Cross (Gal. 6:14); and, further, there is no *real glory* apart from the Cross. Does that sound like a paradox? The Cross is a paradox, inexplicable by the natural mind. The Cross is God's masterpiece.

Seek the power of the Holy Spirit that it may become real to you every day and every moment of the day. Listen again to the apostle Paul:

That I may know Him, and the power of His resurrection, and the fellowship of His sufferings, being made conformable unto His death (Phil. 3:10).

Chapter 5

What is the Significance of *Christ Liveth in Me?*

Christ in You, the Hope of Glory

Here is a wonderful revelation which was locked up in the heart of God for centuries and hidden from the hearts of Old Testament worthies. That is *the mystery that hath been hidden from all ages and generations, but now hath it been revealed to His saints—*to you, my brother and sister*—which is CHRIST IN YOU, the hope of Glory* (Col. 1:26,27). What a stupendous thought, transending our finite comprehension! The Christ of God, *in whom dwelleth all the fullness of the Godhead bodily* (Col. 2:9), condescends to live within the redeemed spirit of a man.

We can conceive of Him as God incarnate, born in the manger, and living as a Man amongst men; we can think of His filling the whole universe with His majesty and glory; we can conceive of His occupying the heavens with all the celestial creation in unquestioning subjection to Him, but to think that He actually condescends to come down and dwell with ME, worm of the dust, is truly beyond human understanding! In fact, it can only be appreciated and realized to any degree by divine revelation (Gal. 1:16). The Holy Spirit causes the indwelling Savior to become a blessed, living realty. *At that day ye shall know that I am in My Father, and ye in Me, AND I IN YOU* (John 14:20).

This wonderful mystery introduces us to the fact that the Lord Jesus still lives in this world. Although He now resides in a different body from that local, physical tabernacle in which He moved in the days of His flesh, He continues His incarnation. You remember how He looked forward, on one occasion,

51

to the time when this great purpose should become an accomplished fact:

> *I have a baptism to be baptized with, and how*
> *am I straitened* (i.e., pent up or held in) *until this*
> *be accomplished (Luke 12:50).*

Although such a mighty and gracious purpose would necessarily involve the sufferings of Golgotha and the death of the cross, the Lord Jesus anticipated *the joy set before Him* when, through that mighty atonement, a glorious release of divine life would become possible (Heb. 12:2).

Since the descent of the Holy Spirit at Pentecost (Acts 2), and down through this age of grace, the primary purpose of God centers round *the formation of this new Body, which is the Church* (Col. 1:24), a spiritual house composed of living stones (1 Pet. 2:5), i.e., all true believers in the Lord Jesus Christ. Wherever a soul has come to the *fount open for sin and uncleanness,* finding peace of heart and life eternal, there is an earthly manifestation of the very life of Jesus (Zech. 13:1). To every heart open to Him the Lord Jesus says, *I will come in* (Rev. 3:20). This heavenly treasure becomes resident in earthly vessels (2 Cor. 4:7). The body of every believer becomes a temple of the Holy Spirit and a vehicle of divine life. *Jesus Christ is IN you except ye be reprobates* (2 Cor. 13:5).

Now let us simply consider two great implications of this wonderful truth. If Christ dwells within you, then:

1. You Become Christ's.

The usurper's authority has been annulled. The Lord Jesus claims you by right of creation and of redemption, has been given possession. A boy made a boat one day from a rough piece of wood with his penknife. Having made it, he lost it. Some time afterwards, to his surprise, he saw this very boat in a shop window. He asked for it, but the shopkeeper claimed it as his own property and said that it could not be surrendered without payment. Putting down the necessary price, the boy walked out with his precious boat once again in his possession, and looking down upon it said, "I *made* you, I *lost* you, I *found* you, I *bought* you; you are mine." So the Lord Jesus redeems His property from the Adversary (1 Pet. 1:18,19). Of every sinner saved by grace He says, "I *created* you, I *lost* you through sin, I *found* you in your need, I *bought* you by blood; YOU ARE MINE." Yes, His residence implies the right of possession.

You are not your own (1 Cor. 6:20). All that you have and are belong to Him. Your body with all its members, your faculties, your talents, your time, your money, your possessions, your heart, your will—all are His! Your very face becomes His to show forth His beauty and glory. Do you remember how the face of Moses shone with the glow of heaven after he had ascended into the mount with God (Ex. 34:29)? This should ever be one of the manifestations of the glorified life. A long-faced Christian is a slander on the joy of the Lord. Victory and joy always go together (Isaiah 12).

Your *eyes* become His to exhibit His sympathy and tenderness. He wants to look on the world's need through your eyes (John 4:35). A Christian should realize this and never lend his eyes to the devil. They belong to the Lord. What a difference it makes when you see things from His point of view!

> Heaven above is softer blue,
> Earth around is sweeter green,
> Something lives in every hue
> Christless eyes have never seen;
> Birds with gladder songs o'erflow,
> Flowers with deeper beauty shine,
> Since I know—as now I know—
> I AM HIS AND HE IS MINE.

Let us yield our *eyes* to Him. In the vilest sinner we shall see a potential saint. You will not see the mote in your brother's eye without discovering that it is the reflection of the beam in your own (Matt. 7:3). Be careful how you use your eyes. They are His; let Him control your vision.

Your *lips* become His to speak His messages (Col. 4:6). This means that the harsh, unkind word remains unspoken.

Others will marvel at the *gracious words which come forth* out of your mouth—even under provocation (Luke 4:22). *Never man spake like this Man* (John 7:46) was the testimony of His enemies, and *this is the Man* who lives within you. In that ministry to which the Lord has called you remember that you are only the instrument for the expression *of His message*. It is not what you say for Him that counts, but what *He says through you* (Is. 55:11) that makes a difference. His words are spirit and life (John 6:63). The Word going forth out of His mouth cannot return unto Him void. Remember, your lips are His. Never lend them to the devil. What havoc has been wrought in many a church and many a life by the cruel gossip-monger and the tattling busybody (Prov. 18:8)!

Your *ears* become His ears. They will be sensitive of every cry of spiritual need. The Savior heard the cry of Bartimeus above the din of the crowd, and in selfless compassion He *stood still* (Mark 10:46), even though the burden of the cross was heavy upon Him. This same Savior lives in you and wants to hear the plaintive cry of the world's need through your ears (Ps. 102:20). Tune in to the bleating of the lost sheep whom the Lord would rescue through you. Never lend your ears to the devil. *Take heed what ye hear* (Mark 4:24). Refuse to hear the voice of the tempter or give your sanction to the spread of false reports and idle rumor concerning others. Your ears are His. As the Lord Jesus ever communed with the Father, so there may be in your life that intimate fellowship with God which enables you to catch His communications day by day.

No tender voice like Thine
Can peace afford.

Your *mind* becomes His, to think His thoughts. It becomes the very *mind of Christ*, because He thinks through you. *Let this mind be in you which was also in Christ Jesus* (Phil. 2:5). Cultivate spiritual thinking. This is the secret of true spiritual discernment, and never was there a day when the Church was in such great need of the Holy Spirit's discernment. Your intellect becomes His that He may plan through you, in order that you might be an instrument for the realization of His purpose. Yield your mind to Him that you may know His secrets and be kept in the current of His will (Ps. 25:14). Never lend your mind to the devil. The mind is his favorite avenue of attack. If the garrison of the mind is captured, the whole citadel falls. A realization of the indwelling Christ and a surrender of your mind and thoughts to Him, is the only remedy for unwholesome thinking and carnal judgments. *Gird up the loins of your mind* (1 Pet. 1:13).

Your *hands* become His to act on His impulse. He will work through you. Again, it is not what you do for Him that counts, but what He does through you (John 5:36). Only that activity which is directly in line of His divine purpose is effective for the kingdom of God. All action is not unction. All endowment is not enduement. Your hands are His. Give them up. Allow Him full use of them, and He will perform His words through your instrumentality. Never lend your hands to the devil. Even Christian hands may commit sin if they slip out of the control of the indwelling Christ.

Your *feet* become His to walk in His way. The Christian's walk is the very walk of Christ. *Walk in love...walk circumspectly* (Eph. 5:2,15). *Walk not as other Gentiles walk* (Eph. 4:17). The feet of the Christian must tread the narrow path the Savior trod, and keep in step with Him throughout the earthly pilgrimage (Gen. 5:24).

Do you see the simple implications of this? In a sentence, YOU ARE HIS. Allow Him to take full possession. Yield your members to His control. Invite Him to allocate your time as His own (Eph. 5:16). Allow Him to energize your talents, your zeal, and your ability with His own resurrection life. You are His by purchase at infinite cost.

Allow Him complete right-of-way through the whole territory of your being—without reserve, without regret, and without retreat. He does not want apartments in your house. He claims the whole building, from the attic at the top to the cellar at the bottom. That is the life of victory. Have you invited Him into every room? What about that sitting room? Does He control that? Is He consulted as to the periods of rest and leisure? What of the reception room and the realm of your friendships (Ps. 119:63)? Are your friends His friends? What about the workroom and the realm of your service? Does He control your activiites and general program? What about the study? Is your reading governed by His tastes (1 Tim. 4:13)? What about the recreation room? Is your recreation consecrated unto the Lord, and are your earthly pleasures sanctified by His sweet presence? Oh, let us surrender the whole house to Him. Is He not worthy of it? Why should we deprive Him of His due?

A reserved compartment in your heart, however small, provides capital for the enemy to work spiritual havoc and rob the believer of victory. Before we pass on to the next phase of this chapter, will you not get to your knees and say again from your heart, "Lord, I surrender all; I give you *the last key.*"?

> Take my life, and let it be
> Consecrated, Lord, to Thee

2. Christ Becomes Yours.

If the fact that you become His implies His possession, then the truth that He becomes yours implies your possession. Have you ever quietly thought this out? Christ is yours!

> Jesus is mine; yes, He is mine—
> Through sunshine and gladness,
> Through sorrow and sadness;
> Jesus is mine; yes, He is mine—
> Forever and ever, my Savior divine.

This means:

a. **His Life Becomes Your Life.** *Christ liveth in me* (Gal. 2:20). *For me to live is Christ* (Phil. 1:21). *Because I live, ye shall live also* (John 14:19). As we have seen, this touches the very vitals of victorious Christian living. The Lord Jesus is not your Helper only, He is your very life.

The victorious Christian life is just the life of the victorious Christ (Rom. 5:10). There is only one Person in the wide universe who can live such a life, and that is *Christ Himself.* It is His life. Since Christ lives in you, however, such a life becomes possible through a human personality. Have you this conception of the Christian life? You cannot get victory by trying to live *for* Jesus. That is the popular way; but very disappointing in its results. Rather it is Jesus LIVING HIS LIFE IN YOU, and that is a very different proposition. The victorious life is His business, not yours. Renouncing the self life gives Him right-of-way to make your heart His palace and His royal throne.

In yourself you cannot live such a life, any more than I can live the life of the Prince of Wales. I have not been born into the Royal Family. If it were possible, however, for the Prince of Wales to clothe himself with my body and live his life in me, then I could live his life. Do you see that? Christ IN you makes victory possible. Christ said, "*Without Me ye can do nothing*" (John 15:5). Therefore, what is the use of trying? No amount of effort can accomplish it. A little girl was stirring her tea furiously and exclaiming, "It's no use, mother, it won't come sweet." And then her mother realized that she had forgotten to put the sugar in! No amount of stirring could make such tea sweet! Yes, His life is your life.

b.   **His Power Becomes Your Power.** This is the power you need. He says, "*All power is given unto Me... Go ye, therefore*" (Matt. 28:18,19). Why? Because He lives in you and places His power at your disposal. You are His instrument, and utterly powerless and impotent apart from Him. He is the great Overcomer (John 16:33). At Calvary, He demonstrated His mighty ascendancy and supremacy over death and Hell, and now He lives in you. His power alone can see you through. Invite Him to ride in triumph through your little city. Face the foe in your own puny strength and you will surely be overcome.

I heard of a speaker who made this point clear to his boy listeners by inviting them all to try and make a pencil stand on its point. Their effort, of course, was unsuccessful, and then he said, "Watch me, and I will show you how to do it". Putting the pencil point downwards on a book, and keeping his finger on the top, he said, "There you are; it is standing on its point". "Oh, but you are holding it," they said. "Yes," he replied, "and that is *how the Christian stands*; he is held and kept by the power of God." That is a simple illustration, but vital in its application. He is able to keep you from falling (Jude 24), and only as you abide in Him are you safe. Lose contact with Him and you fail. This brings us to the next great fact that:

c.   His Victory Becomes Your Victory. Remember, therefore, the triumphant Christian does not fight *for* victory, but *celebrates a victory* already won. This is an important distinction. Have you read 2 Corinthians 2:14 as Conybeare translates it? *Thanks be unto God who leads me on from place to place IN THE TRAIN OF HIS TRIUMPH TO CELEBRATE HIS VICTORY over the enemies of Jesus Christ.* What a magnificent conception of life— to celebrate *His victory!* Because He has conquered, you may be *more than conqueror* (Rom. 8:37). The victory is already won; rejoice in that! All your enemies have been overcome, and the risen, triumphant Lord demonstrates His triumph through those who are joined to Him. With Christ God has given you *all things* (Rom. 8:32).

Imagine a boy returning home after watching his school play football. He shouts to his father, "We won today!" His father turns to him in surprise and says, "We," you say, "and what did YOU do towards it?" The boy replies that he did nothing except look on. Yes, and he was right! "WE won." Somebody else fought the fight. The representative team took the field and won the day, and since this boy belonged to the school, he shared in the victory. No wonder Sambo replied as he did when after his conversion he was asked whether he had the mastery over the devil. "No," he said, "but I have de Master of de devil living in my heart." That is a magnificent theology! Yes, He becomes yours. All that He possesses is at your disposal (1 Cor. 3:21). His victory is your victory.

What is the Significance of *Christ Liveth in Me?*

You have probably heard about the little girl who had a very bad temper. After her conversion, she never again yielded to her temper, and one day she was asked the reason. Her reply was simple and to this effect, "Before the Lord Jesus came into my heart, the devil would knock at the door, and when I went to the door he would push his way in; but now the Lord Jesus has come in, and whenever the devil knocks I say to Him, 'Lord, You go and open the door', and when the devil sees the Lord Jesus at the door he sees somebody who is more than a match for him, and passes on saying, 'Excuse me, I must have come to the wrong house.'" Yes, that is it—Christ IN you.

You are His, and He is yours, and all He asks is for your honest cooperation day by day and moment by moment in His will and purpose for your life. *You must decrease, He must increase* (John 3:30). The last gasp of the self-life will be the first breath of the new. Little wonder is it that the apostle finds his vocabulary limited to describe such an amazing truth, and speaks of *the RICHES OF THE GLORY of this mystery among the Gentiles, which is CHRIST IN YOU, the hope of glory* (Col. 1:27).

I remember hearing of a violinist who came upon the stage one day and gave a wonderful performance. In the midst of the thunderous applause which followed, he did a most extraordinary thing. Lifting his violin high above his head he brought it down with a crash upon a chair and broke it in pieces. The audience listened spellbound for an explanation. "Yesterday," he said, "I gave six shillings and a sixpence for that instrument." Then he disappeared for a few moments and came back with his own violin, an instrument of priceless worth for which he would have exchanged nothing in the world. Again he commenced to play, the same beautiful music, the same exquisite harmony, and only the most highly skilled ear could detect the difference. You see it was not the instrument that mattered, but the master hand that held it. Remember, you are Christ's; and He is yours. Allow His unfettered control of the instrument, and even though you may be conscious of many human limitations, He will bring forth music out of your life. As He places His pierced hands across those human chords, there will emanate a harmony that will cheer His own heart and bring blessing to the multitudes.

In Romania, there is a certain valley where they grow nothing but roses for the Vienna market, and the perfume of that valley in the time of the rose crop is such that if you go into it for a few minutes, wherever you go for the rest of the day people know that you have been there. So may others take knowledge of us as we emanate the fragrance of the indwelling Christ.

Chapter 6

Is It *Sinless Perfection?*

This chapter forms a sort of parenthesis, though its content needs to be carefully considered in connection with the Life of Victory.

Bible teachers who emphasize the need for personal victory in the heart and life of the believer, and who, therefore, teach the way of practical holiness, are often accused of being *sinless-perfectionists.* In fact, it is difficult to avoid this suspicion wherever such a ministry is given. There are always some who assume that the extremes of religious fanaticism are thereby countenanced. Fortunately, a faithful minister of the Word need not be concerned about the opinions or criticisms of others. Indeed, he must always expect some measure of misrepresentation. It is feared, however, that such criticism often arises from prejudice against any stress whatever on practical sanctification in the Christian's walk day by day—and that for reasons of which the critics themselves are most cognizant.

Bible Holiness

It should hardly be necessary to state that the doctine of the Word of God on practical victory is both sane and spiritual. None of us need be afraid of being sinlessly perfect this side of the pearly gates! There is only one sense in which the believer is absolutely perfect at the present time, and that is in his perfect standing before God in Christ Jesus (Heb. 10:14). He is *positionally* perfect; but, as we have seen, he is temporarily residing in a body of humiliation, i.e., a human body beset with limitations and infirmities because of indwelling sin and *flesh*. It is obvious, therefore, that so long as he resides in such a body he cannot reach a state of sinless perfection. There may even be outworkings of that carnality which, although unconscious to the believer himself, constitute defilement in the sight of God. Thank God that the precious blood, in its eternal efficacy, maintains the believer's standing before God and cleanses him from all unrighteousness (1 John 1:7). It should be remembered, however, that *the blood never cleanses the flesh*. The flesh cannot be purified (Jer. 2:22). It must be mortified. This involves *the Cross* aspect of our Lord's atoning death, as distinct from *the blood*. The blood justifies the sinner before God and that eternally (Rom. 3:24). The Cross in its daily application keeps the flesh experientially in the place of death, by the power of the Holy Spirit.

The extreme holiness teaching to which we have alluded, centers round the complete eradication, or destruction, of indwelling sin. As we have seen already, there is no Scriptural authority for such an assertion. The believer is exhorted to *reckon* himself dead to sin. It is obvious that if the flesh is annihilated there is no need for the exercise of such a *reckoning faith*. The whole significance of faith is that it takes an objective or potential fact in Christ and makes it real in experience. Only by this means can it become practical. Cease to exercise faith and it will be quickly discovered that the flesh is present and very much alive. In other words, the root of indwelling sin is still there, but it must not be allowed to *reign* (Rom. 6:12). So long as we live in these bodies, therefore, we cannot be *faultless*.

One day the Church is to be presented *faultless before the presence of His glory with exceeding joy* (Jude 24). Then we shall be sinlessly perfect because we shall be exactly like the sinlessly perfect One, with bodies changed into the likeness of His glorious body.

In the meantime, though, we cannot be *faultless* in that sense; we are called upon to be perfect in the sense of being *blameless* (Phil 2:15). There is a difference. I am not blameable in the sight of God for the presence of indwelling sin. That is a matter of natural generation over which I have no control. I am responsible, however, to appropriate the victory that God offers over all conscious sin, and immediately if I fail to abide in Christ—with its resultant defeat—I become blameable, and need to confess my sin before the Lord. A small boy may write a loving letter to his parents which is full of bad spelling and grammatical mistakes; it is far from faultless, but it may be quite blameless. Do you see the difference?

Further, if there is constant victory in Christ over the resident flesh, what need is there in any case for the extreme teaching of eradication? It cannot provide any more than complete victory over sin, and this is available through a moment by moment reckoning of our crucifixion and resurrection *with Christ.*

Let us beware of an unnecessary, unscriptural, and sometimes dangerous emphasis. Many an advocate of extreme holiness teaching along this line has forfeited the blessed truth of the eternal security of the believer (John 10:28,29). The whole trouble centers around the failure to understand the difference beween the believer's *objective position* in Christ, and his *subjective experience* day by day. It has been accurately put this way: It is not that the believer is NOT ABLE to sin, but that he is ABLE NOT to sin. Let us preach a practical, Biblical holiness. *This is the will of God, even your sanctification* (1 Thes. 4:3). Do not be led astray and injure others by extremes which find no warrant in the truth of Scripture.

The New Life

Chapter 7

How to *Reign in Life*

We now come to the last of our talks, and the climax of the blessed experience of victory in Christ.

> *If by the trespass of the one, death reigned through the one; much more shall they that receive the abundance of grace and of the gift of righteousness REIGN IN LIFE through the One, even Jesus Christ* (Rom. 5:17).

This is something more than the possession of eternal life. It is *life more abundant* (John 10:10). I see a sick young man in hospital. His cheeks are pallid, his eyes are sunken, and his pulse is low. Standing by him is a young man in all the robust vigor of healthy manhood. Each of these possesses life, but in one case it is only a matter of existence; in the other, there is life more abundant. Why should we be content to live poverty-stricken Christian lives when God invites us to appropriate unsearchable riches (Eph. 3:8)? Why should we be spiritual paupers when God's banqueting house is open to us (Song 2:4)? Why paddle in the surf when we are invited to *launch out into the deep* (Luke 5:4)? Our blessed Lord said:

> *He that believeth on Me, as the Scripture hath said, out of his inner man shall flow rivers of living water* (John 7:38).

One day when Robert Annan, the Dundee hero, was speaking about heaven, Mrs. B. said, "I'll be satisfied if I manage somehow to get in." "What?", said Robert, pointing to a sunken vessel that had been dragged up the Tay, "would you like to be pulled into heaven by two tugs like the 'London' yonder? I would like to get in with all my sails set and colors flying."

Let us never be content with a half-blessed Christian experience or be like Ephraim, *a cake not turned* (Hosea 7:8)! God's will is that every one of His children should live up to his income. Why wander in the wilderness when God invites us to journey through a land flowing with milk and honey (Lev. 20:24)? To be a wilderness Christian is to *endure* salvation rather than *enjoy* it. It means a fluctuating joy, a fickle experience, and oftentimes a lack of assurance. I would remind you that the victorious Christian life is not only the possession of eternal life but it is the ACCESSION to the throne. I want to quote to you two further translations of this same text:

> Weymouth: *For if through the transgression of the one individual, death made use of the one individual to seize the sovereignty, all the more shall those who receive God's overflowing grace and gift of righteousness REIGN AS KINGS IN LIFE through Jesus Christ.*

> Moule: *For if in one transgression death came to reign through the one offender, much rather those who are receiving the abundance of grace and free gift of righteousness shall in life (life eternal begun now, to end never) REIGN over their former tyrants through the one, Jesus Christ.*

It was ever God's purpose that man should be a creature of dominion. In Genesis 1, the Church is typified by *the lesser light*, to function as a heavenly body during the period of spiritual night when the sun (the Lord Jesus in His glory) is hidden from the eyes of men. Notice the verb which the Holy Spirit uses to describe this fact. *The lesser light to **rule** the night.* To rule suggests kingly authority. It is a regal privilege. It suggests victory over every foe.

Then, again, the purpose of the creation of man is stated very clearly in verse 26:

*And God said, Let us make man in our image,
after our likeness: and let them have dominion
over the fish of the sea, and over the fowl of the
air, and over the cattle, and over all the earth,
and over every creeping thing that creepeth upon
the earth.*

Man was destined to be a creature of dominion. The three classes of creatures in earth, air, and sea are typical of the believer's threefold enemy in the spiritual realm. *Let THEM have dominion!* Why the change of number to the plural? The next verse explains that they are *male and female*, an authoritative type of Christ and His Church (Eph. 5:32), joined together in holy union.

The Head and Not the Tail

Remember also the injunction and promise to Israel:

*And the LORD shall make thee THE HEAD, and
not the tail; and thou shalt be ABOVE ONLY, and
thou shalt not be beneath* (Deut. 28:13).

There you have the reigning life. *But ye are a chosen generation, a **royal** priesthood (*1 Pet. 2:9a), Peter says. This brings us to the very Alps of Christian experience—*made us sit together in heavenly places in Christ Jesus* (Eph. 2:6). That is your rightful position, my brother or sister. Marvelous truth! Even though we are *earthy* men and women, treading the dusty pathway of life, facing the problems of an earthly pilgrimage, touching *terra firma*, and up against the hard facts of life day by day, our spiritual position, here and now, is *IN THE HEAVENLIES.* This means that we should manifest a heavenly life, radiate a heavenly joy, speak with heavenly language, conduct ourselves with a heavenly demeanor, and sing the heavenly songs. *OUR CONVERSATION* (i.e., CITIZENSHIP) *is IN HEAVEN*, from whence also we look for the Savior (Phil. 3:20). What a salvation, and what a position!

No flesh can enter that realm. Reigning Christians are not incessantly engaged in fighting *the flesh*. No, they have learned the blessed secret of crucifixion, and have been lifted by the Spirit into the glorified life—a new realm of conflict. Their testimony becomes strategic in that sphere where *all things are of God* (1 Cor. 11:12).

This is where the challenge of the evil one becomes a tremendous reality.

> *For we wrestle not against flesh and blood, but against principalities, against powers, against the rulers of the darkness of this world, against spiritual wickedness in high places. Wherefore take unto you the whole armor of God, that ye may be able to withstand in the evil day, and having done all, to stand (Eph. 6:12).*

How the Lord is seeking those who will *STAND* with Him in the conflict, and *REIGN in life* day by day. A carnal believer knows nothing of this. Jordan must yet be passed if he would know the reality of Canaan conflict. No spiritually *strategic* life can be lived on the *flesh level.*

There must be a change of position. Position is power. I heard of a Frenchman who lived in England for some years and afterwards decided to become a naturalized Englishman. He paid the necessary fee, transacted the customary procedure, and became a naturalized Englishman. An old friend ran into him on the following day and said, "Well, I see that now you are an Englishman, but frankly, I don't see much difference in you." Said the one-time Frenchman, "There is a big difference. *Yesterday* the battle of Waterloo was a defeat; TODAY it is a VICTORY!" Yes, and he was right. He had changed his citizenship. That is the heavenly life. A change of position from the realm of the *flesh* into that of the *Spirit*. In that postion, the Lord will turn your *Waterloos* of defeat into *Waterloos* of victory.

Where Do You Live?

The important question is—*Where* are you living? On which level do you normally reside? Are you experientially living in the *heavenly places* day by day? The Savior meant just that when He said, "ABIDE in Me". So *abide* means, Stay where you are. Positionally, you are there. Then ABIDE in Him, moment by moment. Hold your position by faith. The devil will ..... along every subtle avenue to drag you down in spirit—down into depression, down under your circumstances of conditions. Fellow believer, your rightful position is ON TOP (Song of Solomon 4:8). Refuse to come down.

This may necessitate an almost cold-blooded faith, even lifting you above your own *feelings*. Never be governed by your fluctuating feelings. What is true in regard to your salvation is also true regarding your sanctification. Feelings do not count. It is God's FACT that matters. Assert and affirm your position by faith.

I was much impressed some years ago, at a conference of Christians, to hear an aged missionary, recently home from the field, assert that she had often longed to know this heavenly position, but had never been able to get there—or, as she expressed it, to get *within the veil*. One of the Lord's counselors was led to take her to the Word at Ephesians 2:6. He explained that in the purpose of God, she was ALREADY THERE. This was God's fact! There was no need to strive for a position that was hers *already*. *You ARE there; believe it, and take the position, by FAITH.* It was a joy to see the glow that came into her face, and her blessed release of spirit as she recognized that simple truth for the first time, after forty years on the mission field. It is not an act to be performed, or an ideal to be realized, but a fact to be believed. What a blessed realization!

When distributing tracts at a village in the Yorkshire dales, some miles from any railway station, a Christian worker entered the dwelling of a dear old saint of God, eighty-four years of age, who lived alone. One room was all she occupied, and everything in it bespoke the most abject poverty; for if the contents of her apartment had been knocked down at the hammer, the whole would not have fetched more than five shillings. Being desirous of cheering and comforting his aged friend, he remarked to her: "Well, Margaret, soon we shall have done forever with the trials and difficulties of the way, and be fully happy with the blessed Lord Jesus Christ up yonder." "THAT'S MY HOME, SIR," she said. Finding he had begun much below the mark, he sped on, with a view of helping her if possible, and said: "Yes, Margaret, soon we shall be in that bright HOME, the Father's house above, with the Lord Jesus, and around Himself, rejoicing ever in His presence." 'I LIVE THERE, SIR," was her bright and smiling reply. Finding himself still very considerably in the rear, he hastened forward with quickened step, if it were possible, to offer a little help and cheer to his advanced sister in Christ. "How blessed it will be, Margaret—will it not?—when we and all the redeemed, from every clime and of every age, are gathered around the blessed One, who has loved us and washed us from our sins in His own blood; and when we are praising Him together in the glory forever!" "I SING THERE EVERY NIGHT, SIR," was her overwhelming and joyous reply. Thus, his expectations were far more than realized; for instead of helping her, he was cheered and helped himself.

Set Free

Yes, a reigning life is practicable at all times and in all conditions. It is THRONE-UNION with Christ. It is the dominion of *the law of the Spirit of life in Christ* (Rom. 8:2). This alone can liberate from the downward pull of the flesh.

Take another simple illustration. Imagine an airplane on the ground. It is held to the earth by the power of gravity, and is in captivity to that law. Then a pilot approaches, takes his position in that machine, and after some manipulation on levers, etc., that airplane is seen to move upwards and onward. Where is the law of gravity now? Is it abolished or suspended? Of course not. It is still there and is just as powerful as it was before. A new law, however, has taken possession of that machine—a law of life, power, and motion—with the result that it has been lifted above the law of gravity and released from its bondage. If that new law fails to dominate it, the old law again takes possession and down the machine comes to earth.

Now read Romans 8:3:

For the law of the Spirit of life in Christ Jesus hath MADE ME FREE from the law of sin and of death.

Hallelujah! This is the *Reigning Life*. Such a life is pregnant with glorious possibilities. Here alone can be found true joy, heavenly wisdom, and spiritual authority. The Lord would ask each of His children the question put by Jehu to Jehonadab: *"Is thy heart right, as my heart is with thy heart?" And Jehonadab answered, "It is". "If it be, GIVE ME THINE HAND." And he gave him his hand and he TOOK HIM UP TO HIM into the chariot, and he said "COME WITH ME, and see my zeal for JEHOVAH." So they made him RIDE IN HIS CHARIOT* (2 Kings 10:15,16).

Beloved, if our heart condemn us not (1 John 3:21), let us put our own hands afresh into His pierced hand today, and be lifted into His heavenly chariot, and there to share HIS vision and zeal—there to ABIDE moment by moment. This will mean a progressive translation into His image (2 Cor. 3:18), from glory to glory, and such a development into His blessed likeness that *we may have confidence, and not be ashamed before Him at His coming* (1 John 2:28). EVEN SO, may it be!

The New Life

Appendix A

Study Guide

CHAPTER 1

1. How would you paraphrase *the question?*

2. What is the victorious life *not?*

3. The victorious Christian life is a _____, namely _____.

4. Can a true Christian not have the Spirit of God within?

5. What happens when the believer is born again?

6. How much of Christ does the believer receive at salvation? Why is this significant?

7. Why is unceasing victory possible for every believer?

8. Which of the verses listed would be your first choice in pointing someone to Abundant Life?

9. What is God's norm for the Christian life? Why is the common believer's experience abnormal?

10. What are the disciple's three great enemies? Give a definition of each.

11. Is the victorious life burdensome?

12. Which spiritual enemy is internal?

13. Review two Biblical references that identify the devil as a spiritual enemy.

14. What is the difference between *standing* and *state*? Why is this distinction important?

CHAPTER 2

1. By natural birth, everyone is a child of _____.

2. What is the nature of the *inner conflict*?

3. Can sin spring from *the divine nature*?

4. How does Romans 7:15-26 describe this conflict?

5. What is a *carnal* Christian?

6. Show how *flesh* (ethically) does *not* refer to the physical body.

7. What is the relationship between *flesh* and indwelling sin?

8. Why can the flesh not be eradicated during this life-time?

9. Give examples of *good* (religious) flesh.

10. How is flesh related to self-will?

11. Which is wiser: to clean cobwebs or *kill the spider*?

CHAPTER 3

1. When did you learn of this second and deeper aspect of the Atonement?

2. How does the story of the Amalekites in Exodus 17 illustrate the hindrance of the flesh?

3. Wallis defines the deeper work of the Cross: "God saw the end of the old _____, the corrupt _____, and wound it up together as an utterly bankrupt concern.

4. Give two Biblical references that indicate our death with Christ.

5. How does the story of Wyatt and Pratt illustrate identification truth?

6. Give verses that teach the believer's identification with Christ in His resurrection and ascension.

7. What are the three Calvary facts? What do they mean to you?

8. How does the believer appropriate these blessings? By _____.

CHAPTER 4

1. Define *reckoning*.

2. How is reckoning our identification with Christ similar to our salvation experience?

3. What is *the devil's battleground*?

4. Why does sin not have dominion over the believer?

5.   "The Christian does not fight _____ victory
     but stands _____ a victory already won.

6.   What does it mean to you to be *dead to sin?*

7.   The position side of reckoning is that we are _____
     _____ unto _____.

8.   Give Scriptures that show that reckoning is not a once-
     for-all experience.

9.   Why is reckoning more than mental assent?

10. How does John 12:24 illustrate the deeper work of the
     Cross in the believer's life?

11. In what sense is the Cross an "eternal fact"?

12. How do you respond to the issue of complete surrender
     and identification with Christ in His death?

CHAPTER 5

1.   What mystery is revealed to New Covenant believers
     (Col. 1:27)? How can this truth affect your life of dis-
     cipleship?

2.   What is the primary purpose of God in this age—through
     the ministry of the Holy Spirit?

3.   Name two great implications of Christ dwelling in you.

4.   How does Wallis relate the implications of the indwell-
     ing Christ to the believer's daily living? Which of the six
     parts of bodily surrender are most needed in your life?

5.   What are three implication of the blessing "Christ becomes yours"?

6.   Summarize the illustration about the Prince of Wales.

7.   How did a speaker illustrate the need for Christ's power by using a pencil?

8.   How did a young girl appropriate Christ's victory over her bad temper?

9.   Pray or write a prayer expressing your decision to allow Christ to live His life through you (Gal. 2:20).

CHAPTER 6

1.   Why do you think it was important for Wallis to defend the teaching on Christian victory from the allegation of teaching "sinless perfection"?

2.   In what sense is the believer in Christ "perfect"?

3.   How does the teaching of victory in Christ differ from the belief that sin can be eradicated in this lifetime?

4.   Where does the Bible state that Christians will not be totally free from sin until this mortal body is set aside?

CHAPTER 7

1.   What is the difference between being a defeated Christian and "reigning in life" through Christ?

2.   What passage in Romans declares this "reigning" life?

3.   Why is dominion especially appropriate for human be-
        ings (Gen. 1:26)?

4.   Where are believers now seated?

5.   Of what Kingdom are believers citizens?

6.   Why does the nature of the believer's conflict change
        when he "crosses the Jordan" (fully identifies with
        Christ)?

7.   How does living by faith differ from living by feelings?

8.   How does the law of aerodynamics illustrate the law of
        "the spirit of life in Christ Jesus" (Rom. 8:2)?

Appendix B

Definition of Terms as used by Grace Fellowship International

OLD MAN (Old Nature, Adamic Life, Sin Nature)
The unregenerate spirit or Adamic life prior to salvation (Rom. 6:6; Col. 3:9).

NEW MAN
The regenerate spirit, or new nature, consisting of a new human spirit indwelt by the Holy Spirit (Col. 3:10).

FLESH (Self, Self-Life)
A *position* of the non-Christian who is enslaved to the power of sin through the old man. A *condition* of the Christian where the personality is yielded, voluntarily or involuntarily, to the control of indwelling sin which results in living out of human resources.

FLESH (Alternate Definition)
The soul's selfish and distorted perceptions, values, identity messages, and coping mechanisms that have been learned independently of God.

SIN
An unholy force or power which is in me but not me. Sometimes refers to individual acts of sin (1 John 1:7,9; Rom. 7:20).

SINS
Falling short of the mark; violations of God's laws; acts of disobedience (Rom. 3:23; 1 John 3:4).

POSITION AND CONDITION
Position: My true standing. I have a position spiritually of being in Adam or in Christ (Rom. 5:1).
Condition: My condition or state. This condition may or may not reflect my position. It may or may not reflect the truth (Heb. 5:12-14).

IN THE FLESH
A position of the unregenerate man who is in Adam.

AFTER THE FLESH
A statement which may characterize the walk of a Christian. It is allowing sin to control or my living as though I am separate from Christ.

ETERNAL LIFE
Christ's Life. The Life of God which is without beginning or end (1 John 1:1,2; 1 John 5:12)

EVERLASTING LIFE
Life that begins with Adam and will have no end (John 6:47).

IDENTIFICATION
A process of participating in Christ's death, burial, and resurrection which results in an awareness of one's life in Christ as revealed by the Holy Spirit. Awareness comes after experiencing the reality of death or "co-crucifixion" with Christ sometime during one's lifetime. *Every believer is identified with Christ at salvation but may not have appropriated the results of such identification in experience* (Rom. 6:11; 2 Cor. 5:17).

TOTAL COMMITMENT (TOTAL SURRENDER)
A decision of the will, at a point in time, giving God permission to have complete control of one's life. "Reckless abandonment of oneself to God" (Hannah W. Smith). (Rom. 12:1,2).

ACCEPTANCE
The state of being received and totally loved, unconditionally, without personal merit, on the basis of the life and work of the Lord Jesus Christ (Eph. 1:6).

SECURITY
A sure persuasion that I have an eternal, unbreakable, spiritual relationship with God through the Lord Jesus Christ (John 6:37-39).

CARNAL (FLESHLY)
A *position* of the non-Christian who is in Adam and a slave to sin through the old man.
A *condition* of the Christian when he lives by his own resources and has yielded his life, knowingly or unknowingly, to indwelling sin.

TRUTH
What God says...regardless of what I think, feel, or experience (John 8:32).

THE CROSS:

In Redemption: Christ's death for us. Christ's substitutionary sacrifice that purchased the pardon for man's sin (1 Pet. 2:24; Is. 53:6).

In Identification: Our death with Christ. The believer's union with Christ involved the *old man* being crucified. Now the believer's spirit is the *new man* in Christ (Rom. 6:6; Gal. 2:20).

In Consecration: The believer's personal reckoning of his union with Christ. This results in practical freedom from the authority of sin and empowerment by Christ's life (Rom. 6:11; Rom. 5:10).

In Submission: The believer's radical and on-going denial of self and his acceptance of God's will and ways (Rom. 12:1,2; Luke 9:23).

In Liberation: The believer's authority over the flesh (Gal. 5:24), the world system (Gal. 6:14), and demonic forces through Christ's victory at Calvary (Col. 2:13-15; James 4:7).

Appendix C

OUR DEATH AND LIFE IN CHRIST

The Line Diagram (shown on the next page) shows the "life out of death" principle—God's way of disposing of internal conflict. The horizontal line represents eternal life, the life of Christ. By definition, eternal indicates no beginning or end; it exceeds the boundaries of time. Since Christ is God, He has always lived and always will. His life is the "same yesterday, and today, and forever" (Hebrews 13:8). As portrayed at the left of the line, Christ "became flesh" (John 1:14) and lived in a human body for some 33 years. Then, He was crucified, buried and raised from the dead on the third day (1 Corinthians 15:3,4). He continues to live today (Hebrews 7:25). Note that eternal life is not only a present and future reality for the believer but also involves the eternal past.

Until we are born again (John 3:3), we are not in the life of Christ—eternal life—but we are in the spiritually dead life of Adam. One can readily see that if any one of our ancestors, represented by the dots on the diagonal line, had been missing, we also would be missing! Physically speaking, our lives had beginning in Adam, so that whatever happened to him also happened to us. When he sinned, we sinned. When he died (spiritually), we died—just as we would have died in our great-grandfather if he had died before siring any children. Thus, since spiritual death is separation from God, we were all born dead (spiritually). We need forgiveness for our sins, but we also need life. The Lord Jesus Christ came to give us both—by dying for our sins and by giving us His resurrection life (John 10:10).

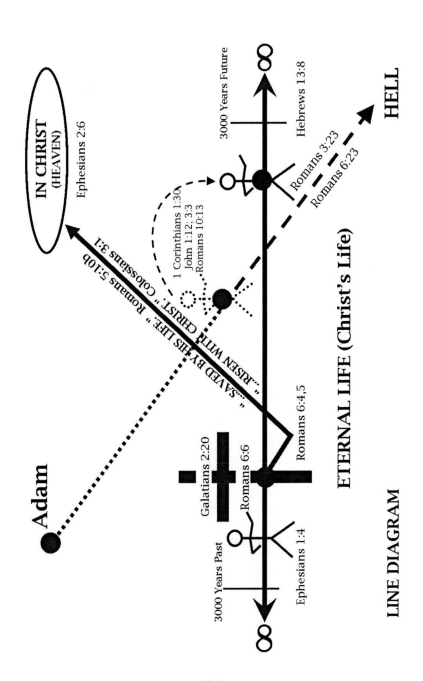

If you are a Christian, you already know this much. What you may not yet know is the following: For the believer, physical death is the gateway from life in the world and the presence of sin to life in Heaven and the presence of God. Similarly, another type of death is the gateway from the sinful life of Adam into the eternal life of Christ. When a person is "born again", he, in the same instant, dies. He is born into the life of Christ, but he simultaneously dies out of the life of Adam. Christ comes into our lives when we believe in Him and are born again, but that is not all; we are also made "partakers" of His life—eternal life. Romans 6:3 says we are not only baptized into Jesus Christ (His life) but also into His death. We can't occupy two opposite lives at the same time—the life of Adam and the life of Christ.

Your Identity

When we receive Christ by faith, it means that His death on the cross counts as payment for our sins. But it means much more. It also means that we enter into a new life—one that extends forever into the past as well as into the future. To put it another way, we exchange our history in Adam—the bad and the good—for an eternal history in Christ. We inherit a new 'family tree'! By becoming partakers of Christ's life, we become participants in His death, burial, resurrection, ascension and seating in the heavenlies (Romans 6:3-6; Galatians 2:20; Ephesians 2:6). He only has one life, and this is the life we receive at our new birth (1 John 5:11,12).

Unless and until we know by personal faith experience that we were crucified with Christ, we will continue to try to live for Christ, using the methods we learned in our old self-lives. The conflicts stemming from our history in Adam will go on plaguing and defeating us. But when, by faith, we take our rightful place at the Cross in union with Christ's death and resurrection, then—and only then—can we truly "walk in newness of life" (Romans 6:4b) where "old things are passed away; behold, all things are become new" (2 Corinthians 5:17).

The Cross experience (understanding experientially our crucifixion and resurrection with Christ) is the gateway into the Spirit-controlled life (Galatians 5:16). It is life out of death, victory out of defeat—the purpose and answer for suffering in the life of the believer. Our path to the Cross, as well as the Cross itself, is a path of suffering; but it is the only path that leads to the end of suffering.

Are you weary enough of your internal conflict and constant defeat to put an end to it by faith? *Are you willing to die to all that you are so you can live in all that He is?* To do so is to exchange the self-life for the Christ-life and be filled or controlled by the Holy Spirit. To refuse to do so is to continue a walk after the flesh and to grieve the Spirit with a continuation of conflict, suffering and defeat.

Salvation Prayer

If you are tired of the anguish that results from doing things your way, Christ will free you if you will sincerely commit yourself to let Him have His way. If you have never accepted Christ as your personal. Savior, your first need is to let God create you anew by giving you spiritual rebirth. You can be born again if you can honestly pray like this:

"Heavenly Father, I have seen that I am a sinner, still in the life of Adam, and that I have committed sins. I believe You sent Your only Son, the Lord Jesus Christ, to die in my place for my sins. I also believe He rose again and now lives, and right now I receive Him into my spirit as my Savior. I surrender all that I am, all I have and all I shall be to You. I turn from my sins and my selfish ways to live my new life in Christ. Thank You for saving me. Amen."

Identification Prayer

If you have prayed the 'salvation prayer', you have been born again, for God says He gives to all who believe in Christ the privilege of becoming His children (John 1:12). Now, whether you prayed for salvation just now or in the past, praying an 'identification prayer' may help you to experience Christ's life of victory and peace. Before this prayer can be effective, you must be truly sick of your self-life; you must be under conviction by the Holy Spirit of trying to live the Christian life in your own strength, and you must be ready to give up control of your life. If this is your condition, pray in this manner.

"Father, thank you for forgiving my sins and taking me out of the life of Adam and grafting me into the life of Christ. Now that I am in Christ, I believe that I was crucified with Him, buried with Him, raised with Him and that I am seated with Him at Your right hand. From this moment on, I choose to have Your Son, Jesus Christ, live His life in me and through me. I consider myself dead to sin and alive to You, and I am counting on the Holy Spirit to make me aware when I forget my death with Christ and try to live His life for Him in my own human wisdom and energy. I choose to yield my total being to You as an instrument of righteousness, allowing no part of me to be used for sin. Thank you for making Christ and His life real to me. Glorify Yourself through me. In Jesus' name I pray. Amen."

Victory is by faith initially and continually. We are saved from *sin* by grace through faith (Eph. 2:8,9), and we are saved from *ourselves* by grace through faith. However, victory *obtained* must result in victory *maintained* through takin gup our Cross daily (Luke 9:23) and continueally (2 Cor. 4:11). It is one thing to take that vital step of being *filled* with the Spirit (Eph. 5:81); but it is equally important that we walk in the Spirit (Gal. 5:17)—a repeated step. It is my prayer that God will use this message to meet you at your point of need and that you, in turn, might be used to His glory in sharing the message of revival with believers and th emessage of salvation witht he lost.

NOTE: For a more complete understanding of the believer's position in Christ and the process of appropriating and maintining vicotry, the reader is refereed to *Handbook to Happiness* (Tyndale House), especially the third edition (1999). The foregoing message is condensed from Chapter 2 of that book by permission of the publisher, all rights reserved.

The New Life

Appendix D

RESOURCES

Books by Dr. Charles Solomon:

Handbook to Happiness
Hacia la Felicidad
Ins and Out of Rejection
Del Rechazo a Aceptación por el Camino de la Cruz
Rejection Syndrome and the Way to Acceptance
Handbook to Happiness & You—A Spiritual Clinic
Handbook for Christ-Centered Counseling
Handbook for Soldiers of the Cross
Handbook to Happiness for the Church—True Revival
For Me To Live Is Christ
The Romans Road—From the Wilderness to Canaan
The Romans Road Tract
Wheel & Line Tract
La Rueda y la Linea (tract)
The Wisdom of (Charles R.) Solomon—
*   Poetry Volumes 1 & 2*
From Pastors to Pastors—Testimonies of Revitalized
*   Ministries*
Discipling the Desperate: The Spirit's Ministry to
*   Hurting Believers*
Gems & Jargon

Books by Dr. John Woodward:

Weekly e-devotional GraceNotes
Blessed Reassurance
Man as Spirit, Soul, and Body

Media Materials:

Conference Audio CDs
Conference DVDs
Conference Notebook

GFI Training:

Exchanged Life Conference
Exchanged Life Workshop
Solomon School of *Spirituotherapy*

Book by Dr. Phil Jones:

How To Exchange Your Life For A New One

Books by Dr. Lee Turner:

Grace Discipleship Course
Advanced Grace Discipleship Course

Book by Captain Reginald Wallis:

The New Life

Resources

For ordering or more information, please contact us at:

GRACE FELLOWSHIP INTERNATIONAL
3914 Nellie Street
P. O. Box 368
Pigeon Forge, TN 37868
(865) 429-0450
www.GraceFellowshipIntl.com

The New Life

CPSIA information can be obtained at www.ICGtesting.com
Printed in the USA
LVOW090143220212

269842LV00001B/4/P